David Lowe
TURGENEV'S
FATHERS AND SONS
Ardis

Copyright ©1983 by Ardis.

Ardis Publishers
2901 Heatherway
Ann Arbor, Michigan 48104

Portions of this book, in altered form, appeared in *Canadian-American Slavic Studies* and *Russian Language Journal.*

Library of Congress Cataloging in Publication Data

Lowe, David Allan, 1948-
   Turgenev's Fathers and sons.

   Bibliography: p.
   1. Turgenev, Ivan Sergeevich, 1818-1883.
Ottsy i deti. I. Title.
PG 3420.O83L68   891.73'3   80-23662
ISBN 0-88233-693-2

CONTENTS

Acknowledgements   7

Introduction   11

A Note on Technical Matters   13

I   Structural Patterns: Parallels and Contrasts   15

II   Characterization in *Fathers and Sons*: Groups   28

III   Characterization in *Fathers and Sons*: Individuals   55

IV   *Fathers and Sons* and the 1860s   82

V   *Fathers and Sons* and Turgenev's *Oeuvre*   103

VI   *Fathers and Sons*: A Quintessential Russian Novel   114

Notes   141

Selected Bibliography   160

ACKNOWLEDGEMENTS

I am obliged to a number of people for their inspiration, advice, and guidance in the preparation of this monograph. Professor Roger Blakely of Macalester College transmitted his enthusiasm for *Fathers and Sons* to me in my undergraduate days. Professor Carl Proffer of the University of Michigan at Ann Arbor initially suggested that it was high time for a doctoral dissertation on Turgenev's novel. The resulting Indiana University dissertation was written under the direction of Professor William B. Edgerton. The thesis committee, all of whose members gave me valuable suggestions and criticisms, included Professors Samuel Fiszman, Andrew Durkin, and Matei Calinescu. Two other colleagues who read the manuscript at the dissertation stage and offered invaluable counsel were Professor Eva Kagan-Kans of Indiana University and Professor Helena Goscilo of the University of Pittsburgh.

In the revising of the dissertation Professor Nina Perlina of Macalester College has been an inexhaustible source of information and insight. I am also indebted to various anonymous readers for the *Slavic and East European Journal, Canadian-American Slavic Studies,* and *Russian Language Journal,* whose criticism of revised chapters from the dissertation and additional research on *Fathers and Sons* has often been extremely helpful.

Needless to say, any errors of fact in the text are my responsibility and mine alone.

FOR INNA VARLAMOVA

INTRODUCTION

There is no shortage of articles and monographs devoted to Turgenev's *Fathers and Sons.* The novel's initial publication in the journal *The Russian Herald (Russky vestnik)* in **1862** provoked a torrent of comment that rushes on unabated even to this day. Much of what has been written apropos of *Fathers and Sons* is valuable and insightful, but there is also a strong undercurrent of biased and largely irrelevant Turgenev criticism, most of it Russian. What distinguishes almost all the existing materials on *Fathers and Sons,* however, is a pronounced one-sidedness. For most of the nearly 120 years that have passed since Turgenev wrote his novel, Russian and non-Russian scholars and critics have tended to concentrate on the topical issues that Turgenev raises, notably Bazarov's nihilism. Until recently, the approach has been more sociological and political than literary. There were always exceptions, of course, but relatively few. Over the last twenty years or so, however, there has occurred an about face in critical stance toward *Fathers and Sons,* especially on the part of non-Russian commentators. There is now a distinct body of criticism of the novel, most of it in English, that sweeps aside socio-politico-historical considerations in favor of a formal or generic approach. This development has been long overdue. What is needed now, however, is an attempt to overcome the present scholarly and critical bifurcation. The fullest appreciation of Turgenev's achievement in *Fathers and Sons* demands a pluralistic approach.

The present monograph attempts a broad examination of *Fathers and Sons* within a variety of frameworks: the novel as an "autonomous" work of imaginative literature, as a reflection of the 1860s, as a part of Turgenev's *oeuvre,* and as a work of Russian literature. The material is not always organized strictly according to this catalogue of contexts, but the listing provides the overall framework within which I have chosen to work.

The first three chapters are devoted to *Fathers and Sons* as a work of imaginative literature. These chapters, which are organized around the topics of structure, characterization, and imagery, deal with the novel largely in formal terms, always with an eye to their implications for interpretation of the novel. The section on *Fathers and Sons* as a reflection of the 1860s deals with the novel's historical background.

Most of the remarks about *Fathers and Sons* as a work by Turgenev are aimed at showing how atypical the novel is for a Turgenev narrative. Though of course is displays formal and thematic similarities with other Turgenev works, it is in a variety of ways the grand exception within the context of Turgenev's *oeuvre.*

The final chapter treats *Fathers and Sons* as a work that occupies a central position in the evolution of the Russian novel. In *Fathers and Sons* Turgenev both draws upon and further develops themes and techniques introduced into Russian literature by the most outstanding of his predecessors–Pushkin, Lermontov, and Gogol. Moreover, just as Turgenev's novel is a reflection of the major works of Russian literature preceding it, so also is it a signpost indicating the directions the Russian novel was to take in the hands of his successors.

The importance of *Fathers and Sons* has been at times underestimated, at times misunderstood because critics are apt to treat the novel within too limited and too limiting a context. I have undertaken herein to attempt to improve the state of Turgenev scholarship by providing a variety of contexts within which we may profitably discuss *Fathers and Sons.*

A NOTE ON TECHNICAL MATTERS

The basic source for Turgenev's works is I. S. Turgenev, *Polnoe sobranie sochinenii i pisem v 28-i tomakh* (M-L, 1960-1968). This edition is divided into two sets of volumes: works *(sochineniia)* and letters *(pis'ma)*. References to *Fathers and Sons* will be indicated by a single arabic numeral. Such references refer to Volume VIII of the works, where the text and variants for *Fathers and Sons* are to be found. In other references a roman numeral followed by a comma indicates letters. The twelfth volume of letters is subdivided into two volumes, as is the thirteenth: they will be indicated by a subscript. Thus, (325) indicates page 325 of Volume VIII of works; (X, 276) refers to page 276 of the tenth volume of works; and (12_1, 265) indicates page 265 of the first part of the twelfth volume of letters.

All translations are my own unless otherwise noted.

I

> If we find in *Fathers and Sons* a sad poetry of life, it is because so often Turgenev is in tune with the underlying rhythm of life, the flowering and the fading, of love, ideals, and of ourselves. But in all this, as in the flowers which cover Bazarov's grave, there is a constant faith in the continuity and the purpose of ordinary life—and wonder at its perpetual mystery.[1]

STRUCTURAL PATTERNS: PARALLELS AND CONTRASTS

Sometime during the first months of 1862 Afanasy Fet sent Turgenev his reactions to *Fathers and Sons.* Fet's letter is not extant, but we do have Turgenev's reply, and it reinforces the often expressed conviction that one ought not to pay too much attention to what writers have to say about their own works. In the letter of April 6/18, 1862, Turgenev writes: "You also mention parallelism; but where is it, allow me to ask, and where are these pairs, believing and unbelieving?" (4, 371). The second part of Turgenev's question will be addressed in the next chapter, which deals with characterization in *Fathers and Sons.* The groundwork for that chapter will be laid in the present one, where it will be demonstrated that in spite of Turgenev's protests parallelism is one of the two basic principles at work in the novel. The other is contrast. No doubt there are few works in world literature that do not depend to some extent on parallels and contrasts for the building blocks that hold them together and give them coherence. In *Fathers and Sons,* however, their significance is all-inclusive and extends to matters of composition, characterization, and thematics. In *Fathers and Sons,* a novel whose very title both links and contrasts the generations, form and content are one. That pronouncement is not the pious repetition of a Formalist cliché. As the examination proceeds it should become increasingly apparent that in *Fathers and Sons* thematics determine form. As the first step in proving the validity of that contention, let us turn our attention to matters of composition and their relation to the novel's thematic concerns.

One way to look at the novel's structure is as a series of trips: Arkady and Bazarov are thus examined and illuminated in a variety of environments. At Marino Arkady is at home and Bazarov is the stranger. In town and at Nikolskoe, both Arkady and Bazarov are thrown into an unfamiliar environment, while at Bazarov's parents' estate Arkady is the stranger (though, paradoxically, he is less an outsider there than is Bazarov). Parallelism and contrast are immediately evident in such a scheme: Bazarov is the newcomer in one milieu, Arkady in another. But even within the series of trips we can establish cycles. Brazhe writes of two cycles of trips from Marino to Bazarov's home.[2] Such a calculation takes into account only Bazarov's point of view. It would be more accurate to identify three cycles of trips. The interesting structural note here is that Arkady's and Bazarov's travels consistently dovetail with each other, even when the two protagonists are not together. In the first cycle, Arkady and Bazarov go from Marino to town to Nikolskoe to Bazarov's home and back through Nikolskoe to Marino. In the second cycle, Arkady goes to Nikolskoe on his own. In a later and parallel development, Bazarov arrives at Nikolskoe on his own. Finally, in the last cycle, Bazarov goes home alone, as does Arkady. Implicit in this view of the novel's structure is one of the novel's major themes: children cannot turn their backs on the world of their fathers. Imperfect as it may be, it represents the mainstream of humanity. Children ultimately do go "home" again, and willingly or grudgingly, they are reconciled to the family hearth. At that point, as Joel Blair notes, "the lives of the fathers become patterns for understanding the lives of the children."[3]

A second way of viewing the structure is as a series of confrontations. Such an interpretation is particularly widespread, since it provides abundant opportunities to discuss the ideological battles of the 1860s. Thus, we can map out the structure of *Fathers and Sons* as a series of ideological duels between Bazarov and Pavel, the ideological duels then capped by a real duel in which politics and social issues are as much at stake as personalities.[4] Doubling the ideological skirmishes is Bazarov's series of erotic clashes with Odintsova.[5] All discussions of the structure of *Fathers and Sons* in terms of confrontations are ultimately spinoffs from

Gippius' Formalist analysis of composition in Turgenev's novels.[6] (Rarely are they acknowledged as such.) Gippius' analysis is quite sophisticated, and there will be a need to return to it in some detail. It is nonetheless limited because, like most analyses of *Fathers and Sons,* it proceeds from the assumption that the novel is a tragedy and that Bazarov is the novel's only significant protagonist. These assumptions lead critics to attempt to identify a single, all-embracing structural pattern in the novel, whether it be trips, confrontations, love stories, or whatever. But the assumption needs to be reexamined. *Fathers and Sons* is a novel wholly dependent upon parallels and contrasts for its composition, and its structure is dualistic: it involves two parallel but contrasting patterns. The first is that of tragedy, while the second is comedy.[7]

Since many will probably find controversial the notion that *Fathers and Sons* is in any way comedic, let us begin with this, the less obvious structural pattern in the novel. In using the word comedy, what it intended is not comedy in the popular sense (a funny play with a happy ending), but in the Aristotelian sense, specifically in its modern formulation by Northrop Frye. Frye uses comedy as a term denoting a literary mode, as he calls it, not a genre. Thus, as defined by Frye, the term is equally applicable to drama and narrative prose.

Basing his treatise on Aristotle's *Poetics,* Frye suggests that comedies deal with the integration of society. The standard comedic formula involves a young couple—the technical hero and heroine—whose marriage is blocked by other members of the cast (society). In realistic fiction employing the comedic mode, the hero and heroine tend to be dull but decent people, while the blocking characters are the truly interesting ones. The blocking characters are normally, but not necessarily, parental figures. They are consumed by a single passion (usually absurdly so), and they are in control of the society into which the hero and heroine seek entrance. The blocking characters are likely to be impostors, as Frye calls them, people who lack self-knowledge. At the conclusion of comedy the blocking characters are either incorporated into or expelled from the society, as a result of which the hero and heroine are free to wed. Thus, comedies often conclude with a wedding and the birth of babies, and have a rural setting (an escape to a simpler, less corrupt society). At the conclusion of comedy the audience feels that justice has triumphed, that the people who should have been united have been, and that everyone will live happily ever after in a freer, more flexible society.[8]

This is a rather bald reduction of Frye's Aristotelian description of comedy, but it should be sufficient to demonstrate that in *Fathers and Sons* we are dealing in part with the comedic mode. However, Turgenev spins some fascinating variations around the age-old comedic pattern.

Arkady is the technical hero about whom the comedic plot revolves. This is not to say that he is the novel's central hero. He is the *technical* hero of the comedic plot.[9] Significantly, Gary Jahn notes that "Arkady *and* Bazarov are the organizational focus of the novel [Italics mine–DL]."[10] And true to comedic type, Arkady is a rather bland but not unattractive personality. As in Roman comedy, we have not a single hero, but a pair of heroes. Instead of the typical pair of young heroes, however, Turgenev gives us a father and son, both of whose marriages are blocked, as is a genuine reconciliation between father and son. The blocking characters are Pavel and Bazarov, and consistent with the traditions of fictional comedy, both of them are considerably more interesting than the technical heroes and heroines, and both of them are removed from the stage at the culmination of the comedic plot line.

Bazarov's negative influence on Arkady forestalls an accomodation between him and his father, and it temporarily blocks Arkady and Katya's marriage, largely because Bazarov's attitudes, which Arkady attempts in vain to adopt, prevent the latter from coming to terms with himself and his true nature. In this connection, James Justus points out that "the battle [in *Fathers and Sons*] is not just fathers against sons, but sons against themselves."[11] Bazarov's obstructing influence is apparent as early as the third chapter. Arkady, riding along in a carriage with his father, waxes lyrical, thus betraying his "unnihilistic" enthusiasm for the beauties of nature. He abruptly breaks off in mid-sentence. "Arkady suddenly paused, glanced back obliquely [at Bazarov, who is riding along behind] and lapsed into silence" (203). Bazarov's presence prevents Arkady from being himself, and as a result the relations between father and son are strained. Bazarov is a blocker, and his status as an obstacle to reconciliation between father and son is emphasized in several of the novel's passages. Just after the scene in which Bazarov suggests that Arkady wean his father away from Pushkin by giving him more adult food for thought, i.e., Büchner's *Stoff und Kraft* (sic) (238-239),[12] we discover Pavel and Nikolay in conversation:

> "Well, you and I," Nikolay Petrovich, sitting in his brother's room the same day after dinner, said to Pavel, "have fallen into the ranks of the retired, our song is sung. What's to be done? Perhaps Bazarov is right; but I confess that one thing pains me: I was hoping just now to become close friends with Arkady; but it turns out that I have lagged behind, he has gone forward, and we cannot understand each other." (239)

By the end of the novel there is no doubt that it is precisely Bazarov's sway over Arkady that temporarily thwarts mutual understanding between father and son. Furthermore, Arkady's distorted image of himself as a fire-breathing, militant disciple of Bazarov's impedes his progress toward the realization that his love is not for Odintsova, as he imagines, but for her sister Katya. It is Katya who articulates what the reader has sensed all along—Arkady has been under Bazarov's thumb. "My sister was under his [Bazarov's] influence then, just as you were" (364), Katya tells Arkady. She goes on to inform Arkady that he has nothing in common with Bazarov. When Arkady protests, saying that he wants to be strong and energetic like his friend, Katya lectures him: "You can't just wish that... Your friend does not wish for it, it's just there in him" (365). Here Katya sounds another of the novel's major themes: one cannot be what one is not. That Arkady's attempt to play the nihilist causes him to be untrue to himself is made explicit when Bazarov suggests that they go to town:

> "...Well, what do you think? Shall we go?"
> "I guess so," Arkady answered lazily.
> In his soul he rejoiced at his friend's suggestion, but felt obliged to hide his feeling. Not for nothing was he a nihilist! (252)

Arkady's transition from his false role as Bazarov's protegé and a rival for Odintsova to his true status as his father's son and claimant for Katya's hand is signalled in a scene at Nikolskoe:

> They did not find him [Arkady] soon: he had taken himself off to the most remote part of the garden where, resting his chin on his folded hands, he sat, sunk in thought. [Cf. Nikolay's penchant for garden meditation.] They were profound and important, these thoughts, but

> not sad. He knew that Anna Sergeievna was sitting alone with Bazarov, and he did not feel jealousy, as had happened in the past; on the contrary, his face shone quietly; it seemed that he was surprised at something and gladdened, and that he was deciding on something. (373-74)

It is appropriate that Arkady should come to such self-knowledge in the garden. Alexander Fischler has noted that the architecture of *Fathers and Sons* is linked to a garden motif, and that "the garden is a microcosm of nature, foreshortening its laws to uphold *what ought to be*."[13] Arkady's post-garden proposal to Katya is a symbolic declaration of what he must be—independent from Bazarov: Arkady is now free to be himself, to express his true feelings. Bazarov's dramatic farewell and rejection of Arkady are really no more than a recognition on the former's part that he no longer has any influence over Arkady. Bazarov then retires to his father's house, removing himself from the comedic plot line and freeing Arkady to marry Katya and to be reconciled with his father.

Pavel is a blocking character vis-à-vis Nikolay and Fenechka. His presumed hostility to the idea of their marriage dissuades Nikolay from regularizing his liaison with Fenechka. Note Nikolay's reaction when Pavel asks him to marry Fenechka:

> Nikolay Petrovich took a step back and threw up his hands. "Is that you saying this, Pavel? You, whom I have always considered an implacable foe of such marriages? ... But don't you know that it was only out of respect for you that I haven't fulfilled what you so rightly call my duty!" (362)

So Pavel encourages Nikolay to marry Fenechka--an act that will assuage Nikolay's guilty conscience and allow him to feel more at ease with his son.

Then, at the culmination of the comedic plot line the blocking characters have been expelled (or have expelled themselves): Pavel prepares to spend the rest of his days in Europe, where he will continue his superfluous existence, while Bazarov retires to his father's home, and the pairs who belonged together all along are at last united.

Some critics have noted the importance of couplings, uncouplings, and recouplings in the novel. Reeve writes:

> Characters in pairs ... relate each to the other through a succession of

still other people, each relationship forming a temporary triangle, each triangle imperfect . . . . The third person's action always in some sense splits the original pair.[14]

Or, as Blair formulates it:

The principle of composition operating in the novel is the grouping and regrouping of characters; our understanding of the novel develops as we observe the initial groups of characters dissolve and perceive the formation of new pairs. Eventually, those characters who seemed most unalike are aligned; their similarities become more important than their differences.[15]

This general movement toward the final, "inevitable" pairings is the stuff of comedy. The double wedding noted in the epilogue underscores the emergence of a new, pragmatically freer society, a salient feature of comedy. The crystallization of this less rigid society is underlined by Pavel when he urges Nikolay to marry Fenechka: "No, dear brother, enough of high-mindedness and thinking about society: we're already old and peaceful people; it's time we put aside empty pretense" (362). The new society, though not earthshakingly different from the old, is a little less rigid, a little more spontaneous: Nikolay, a member of the gentry, has become free to take Fenechka, a peasant, as his lawfully wedded wife. In this respect Shklovsky overstates the case in arguing that "What is new in Turgenev's novel was that he understood the love story as the confrontation of new people with a world built on old principles."[16] It is really Nikolay and Fenechka who confront old social values with new ones, Arkady and Katya's thoroughly conventional marriage with their own socially "progressive" one. Shklovsky's assessment nonetheless shows that he perceives a comedic base in the novel. Fischler, who emphasizes the classical bases of *Fathers and Sons*, also sees comedy at work here. He writes of the epilogue as *"prostodushnaia komediia,* 'artless comedy'—life itself or a play in which the author's strings no longer matter. In such comedy, the naive pursuit of happiness by the characters remaining on the stage blends with the timeless designs, overwhelming what momentarily stood out and was disturbing because of its alien, fortuitous or fateful appearance."[17]

What are the implications of the novel's comedic structure? One, obviously, is that the comedic mode is extraordinarily hardy and adaptive. But, more importantly, an analysis of *Fathers and Sons* in terms of comedy explains in generic terms why many critics read the novel as an affirmative one—one that celebrates life and nature (or, more accurately, Life and Nature). Strakhov, for instance, argues: "Although Bazarov stands above everyone in the novel, life stands above him."[18]

But what kind of life stands above Bazarov? Some critics dismiss the life led by Katya, Arkady, Nikolay, and Fenechka as banal, mediocre, *poshly*.[19] Pisarev, for one, suggests: "The life of a limited person always flows more evenly and pleasantly than the life of a genius or even just an intelligent person."[20] Byaly asserts that Pavel and Nikolay are "finished" *(konchenye liudi),* that "life is passing them by."[21] (Byaly is wrong to equate Pavel with Nikolay, by the way. The distinction between the brothers will be taken up in the next chapter.) Thus, for Byaly, Nikolay is not even involved in life.

Do Nikolay and Arkady and their wives represent mediocrity? Yes, but not in a negative sense. Their mediocrity is that of the middle way, the golden mean. Arkady and Nikolay may be ordinary, but, as Paul Bourget suggested, nearly a century ago, there is something fresh and appealing about Turgenev's average man.[22] Turgenev himself spoke of Goethe's Faust as the defender of "the individual, passionate, limited man" who still has the right and the opportunity to be happy and not be ashamed of his happiness" (I, 235). Boyd writes: "The love of Arkady and Katya gives a healthy, optimistic balance to the novel."[23] Batyuto calls the novel's love scenes life affirming.[24] And Vinogradov writes:

> The novel in essence is a battle of "cerebral" negative theories with the mighty power of love, with the inexpressible beauty of nature, with all the intermix of human feelings which, though "old," are alive and warm—a battle that ends with the triumph of "humanness," "nature," "beauty," over "nihilism."[25]

The comedic couples may be limited, but they are hardly vegetables, nor is their existence gray. Arkady is a competent estate manager,[26] and all the Kirsanovs' lives, ordinary as they may be, are enriched by an instinctual and profound attraction to nature, art, and their fellow man. They represent an ideal that Turgenev himself was unable to attain. While working on *Fathers and Sons,* he wrote a letter to K. N. Leontiev in which he confessed:

> And that I, as you write, have lately become gloomy, there's nothing surprising in that: I will soon be 42 years old, but I haven't made a nest for myself, haven't secured any spot for myself on earth: there is little cause for joy in that. (4, 136)

It must be admitted, however, that Turgenev claimed *(post-facto)* that in *Fathers and Sons* he had taken a contemptuous, despairing attitude toward bourgeois domesticity. In a letter of April 14/26, 1862, to Sluchevsky, Turgenev responds to what seems to have been Sluchevsky's summary of the reactions of Russian students in Heidelberg to *Fathers and Sons* (no letters from Sluchevsky are extant). The students' reactions are indicative, as is Turgenev's reply:

> What was said about Arkady, about the rehabilitation of the fathers, etc., only shows—forgive me!—that I haven't been understood. *All my povest*[27] *is directed against the gentry as a progressive class.* Examine closely Nikolay Petrovich, Pavel Petrovich, Arkady. Weakness, flabiness *(vialost)*, or limitedness *(ogranichennost)*. (4, 380)

Later in the same letter Turgenev expresses bewilderment at the Heidelberg students' having found Arkady "a more successful type [than Bazarov]" (4, 380). Thus we have Turgenev's own testimony that he did not intend to portray Arkady or Nikolay in a positive light. But an author's intentions are one thing, the reader's perceptions quite another. In spite of scornful depictions of "blissful" marriages in other Turgenev works, such as "Andrey Kolosov," "Two Friends," and "The Country Doctor," and Turgenev's protestations to the contrary, Nikolay, Arkady, and their wives add a healthy, optimistic note to *Fathers and Sons*. In this connection Gippius, discussing groups of *poshlye* characters in *Smoke* and *Nest of Gentlefolk*, points out that these characters are "portrayed with exaggerated distortion, not at all as in *Fathers and Sons*, where the corresponding characters are presented in a significantly muted *(smiagchenny)* form, almost idealized, no matter how much Turgenev himself denied it."[28]

Arkady and Nikolay are not men of great stature, they are not great thinkers, but Turgenev's having infused them with love of Schubert, Pushkin, evening sunsets, their families, and their fellow man makes it difficult to conceive of them and the life they lead as *poshly*. Turgenev portrays the Kirsanovs in a positive, if subdued light. And he does so within the context of a comedic structure, one that invariably leads the audience at the conclusion to recognize that "this is how things ought to be." Bazarov's death is quite another matter, of course. That is the culmination of the novel's tragic structure. But in the first part of the novel's epilogue, where life and love are celebrated at Pavel's farewell dinner, with its exaltation of marriage and family, "Turgenev stands for the eternal foundations of human life, for those basic elements which may perpetually change their forms, but in essence always remain unchanged."[29]

But of course not all critics find such positive notes in *Fathers and Sons.* Most would probably argue that the novel is a tragedy. Such an analysis should surprise no one—it is a bromide of Turgenev criticism. But how and why *Fathers and Sons* is a tragedy—these are questions that until recently have remained largely unexplored.[30] Once again Northrop Frye provides useful tools for analysis.[31] The basic movement of tragedy, according to Frye, is toward the exclusion of a hero from a given society, with an emphasis on the hero's tragic isolation. It is in this connection that Gippius' analysis of the structure of *Fathers and Sons* is particularly apt. He perceives the novel's "dynamic highway" in this way: "Having cast himself off from the elements of his milieu, the obviously hostile ones as well as the pseudo-friendly ones, the hero remains tragically alone."[32] Yury Mann sees a similar pattern, which he calls "one against all."[33]

According to Frye, the tragic hero must be of heroic proportions: "The tragic hero is very great as compared with us, but there is something else, something on the side of him opposite the audience, compared to which he is small."[34] Surely this is the case with Bazarov, whose greatness (implied, rather than shown) is, as Strakhov argues, less than the sum of life forces represented by the Kirsanovs and their spouses.[35]

In addition, Frye conceives of the tragic hero as an impostor, someone who is deceived about himself, who plays a role that is not his to play. Significantly, Charles Bachman writes of "tragedy and self-deception" in *Fathers and Sons,* pointing out that "false self-images are crucial to the tragic view which the action of the novel seems to demand . . . ."[36] Most of the characters in the novel suffer from identity crises: this is true not just in the case of the strong characters, as Bachman suggests, but also of such a person as Arkady. But Bazarov's self-deception is the most extreme and his journey toward self-discovery the most painful and tragic. He dismisses the laws governing human life; his fatal infection, leading him to summon Odintsova for a last meeting in which he confesses that he is not the giant he had imagined himself to be, demonstrates that finally he understands the extent of his self-delusion.

The movement toward tragedy is generally toward a revelation of natural law, "that which is and must be,"[37] so that the audience's reaction to the hero's fall is paradoxical: we feel a sense of rightness (the tragic hero represents an imbalance in nature and thus must fall) and horrible wrongness (how sad that this man must fall). Such indeed is our reaction to Bazarov's death. Poignant as it may be, we nevertheless perceive, as Richard Freeborn formulates it, that Bazarov is a

> usurper of divine right, whose arrogant self-will proclaims for itself a self-sufficiency in life which contravenes the limits of human experience and gives rise to a dilemma which is only to be resolved in death.[38]

Fischler's approach to the question of Bazarov throws additional light on Turgenev's reliance on classical tragedic models:

> One must first note that Bazarov belongs to a special category of protagonists, the tragic protagonist or even the nature hero. He fits there less because of his famous assertion that nature is his "workshop," than because of his repeatedly underlined mysterious bonds with his natural surroundings. He is associated with nature not only by brute strength and passion, but by vaguer, though not necessarily less awesome bonds of sympathy: the world responds to him, follows him, at least so long as he chooses to practice and accept association, that is, throughout the first part of the novel. He is born with a gift for harmony with the creation, yet, as he himself points out to Arkady, it is a gift of limited usefulness: one may derive strength from nature so long as one yields to it through naive faith, so long as one is willing to believe in the talismanic virtue of an aspen tree by a clay pit; but, when the magic is lost, one must drift to the inevitable end. Nonetheless, even when Bazarov's bond to nature ceases being a means for coping with the world, his fate remains associated with it by the structure of the novel. He is a nature hero, and, by ironic extension, he is even a nature "god"; he appears on the stage in spring (May 1859) to offer the traditional challenge to an existing order already undermined by inner and outer turmoil; he is defeated (expect perhaps in the duel with Pavel Kirsanov, the living-dead

representative of the older order who, in many respects, is a projection of himself); then, largely through his own acquiesence and even complicity, he dies in August, at the height of summer, a traditional time for the death of gods . . . .[39]

Comedy and tragedy coexist in *Fathers and Sons.* It is of course the novel's tragic side that impresses us most deeply. Such is human nature. Moreover, Turgenev takes pains to reinforce the novel's tragic overtones by placing the description of Bazarov's aged parents weeping inconsolably at their son's grave as the last element in the novel, the final chord of a tragic symphony, as it were. And yet, if we look closely at the very last lines of *Fathers and Sons,* we see that the narrator holds out a certain note of optimism, ambivalent as it may be:

> Can it really be that their prayers and their tears are fruitless? Can it really be that love, sacred, devoted love is not all-powerful? Oh no! No matter what a passionate, sinful, rebellious heart may be hidden in the grave, the flowers that grow on it look at us serenely with their innocent eyes; they speak to us not only of eternal peace, of that great peace of "indifferent" nature; they speak as well of eternal reconciliation and of life eternal.... (402)

But what does Turgenev mean by "life everlasting"? The life of nature, which renews itself annually? The life of humanity, which is everlasting inasmuch as a new generation always takes the place of the dying one? Does the narrator really have in mind the Christian notion of the immortality of the soul? He is purposely vague in this quasi-pantheistic, quasi-Orthodox formulation. What is clear is that life goes on. Bazarov is dead, but Nikolay and Fenechka, along with Arkady and Katya, are multiplying and bringing forth much fruit.[40]

The novel's tragic side predominates, but it does not overwhelm. Significantly, critics who write of *Fathers and Sons* as a tragedy often stop short of calling it a tragedy, pure and simple. Charles Bachman calls it "a basically tragic novel."[41] Helen Muchnic descibes the novel as "tragic in its implications, but not in its tone."[42] Such hesitation can be accounted for on the formal level by the recognition of coexisting comedic and tragic modes within the novel.[43] Observing this relationship helps us to understand —in formal terms—the initial and continuing furor created by

Fathers and Sons. In "Apropos of *Fathers and Sons*" Turgenev writes that he has an interesting collection of documents and letters from readers who accuse him of doing totally contradictory things in his novel (XIV, 104). This is hardly surprising, since Turgenev *is* doing what seem to be contradictory things within the work. By combining the tragedic and comedic modes he seems to stand behind two diametrically opposed views of life at one and the same time. If we take the novel's comedic structure out of context, we conclude that life is triumphant, rewarding, and meaningful. Such is the conclusion that any comedy forces upon us. And in *Fathers and Sons* the portraits of the Kirsanovs, their babies, their joyful participation in the natural cycle, all lead the audience to infer that all's right with the world. On the other hand, if we take the novel's tragedic side out of context, we are led to the view that life, which is ruled by fate and the irrational, is essentially meaningless: death is triumphant. Where does Turgenev stand? "Where is the truth, on which side?" we may ask, as does Arkady (324). And Bazarov's answer is most appropriate: "Where? I'll answer you like an echo: where?" (324). An analysis of the novel's dualistic structure shows that the truth is on both sides. Or, as Fischler argues, the problems raised in *Fathers and Sons* are insoluble and the rifts revealed can be mended only by time.[44] This conclusion is supported by one of Turgenev's letters to Annenkov, in which he writes: "I know that in nature and in life everything is reconciled one way or another... If life cannot [do the reconciling], death will reconcile" (2, 144). Thus Turgenev's own view of life is dualistic, but not contradictory, and this dualism lies at the heart of *Fathers and Sons:* as we have seen in this chapter, it accounts for the novel's structure. In the next chapter we will see that it is also the basic principle underlying characterization in the novel.

II

CHARACTERIZATION IN *FATHERS AND SONS:* GROUPS

There is an ambiguity inherent in the term "characterization." For some critics it implies the formal methods by which an author creates the illusion of living personages within a work of fiction. Used in this sense, the notion of characterization presumes a desire on the critic's part to intuit his way into the author's psyche, to describe what processes are involved in the author's selection and organization of his materials—even if, as is usually the case, the author professes no knowledge of such matters. For other critics, however, characterization concerns not the creation of personalities, but their interpretation. In this case a critic looks at a work not from the viewpoint of a writer, but from that of a reader, usually one who is interested in psychology or philosophy. And between these two positions there is an often unrecognized abyss.

In view of this potential for confusion, it is essential to try to formulate at the outset exactly what will be dealt with in these chapters on characterization in *Fathers and Sons*. Broadly speaking, this chapter and the next focus on the nature of the information Turgenev provides about characters in *Fathers and Sons*, how it is relayed, the patterns of its transmission, and how it guides our perceptions of characters and character. In other words, the working definition of characterization here is broad—it takes into account both methods and implications. Characters and character in *Fathers and Sons* will be illuminated from as many angles as possible and to that end we will be dealing with a variety of interrelated topics, including matters that strict formalists would probably classify as elements of narration, style, and imagery, rather than characterization.

Broadly speaking, the two major sources of information about characters in *Fathers and Sons* include (1) information that any given character provides about himself and (2) information provided by other characters and the narrator. If we begin with the second group of sources, we can distinguish three general types of information about characters in *Fathers and Sons:* (a) what seem to be minimally evaluative, maximally objective surface descriptions of appearance, actions, and reactions, (b) overtly evaluative remarks about behavior, and (c) information relating to heredity and environment.

Surface descriptions tend to focus on hair, facial expression, clothing, and body language. Such descriptions are not applied in equal measure to all characters. If Arkady, Nikolay, and Katya seem pale, for instance, that is for a good reason: we learn relatively little about their looks. They are literally rather faceless characters. (Note that this is entirely in keeping with their function as comedic heroes and heroines.) Details of dress are everywhere important, especially in the case of Bazarov and Pavel. Bazarov's and Pavel's contrasting modes of dress—the former's lack of attention to it, the latter's fastidious concern for his toilette—are very much reflections of the essence of their personalities.

Kurlyandskaia makes some very apt observations about Turgenev's descriptions of actions and reactions. First, she points out that in Turgenev's world, the more intense a character's emotions, the more immobile his response.[1] The examples that she gives are from *A Nest of Gentlefolk,* but several instances in *Fathers and Sons* come immediately to mind. When Arkady first announces that Bazarov is a nihilist, Pavel freezes:

> "What?" asked Nikolay Petrovich, and Pavel Petrovich poised his knife in the air with a piece of butter on the tip of the blade and remained immobile. (215)

Or consider Bazarov's state just after his declaration of love for Odintsova: "Odintsova extended both her hands to him, but Bazarov pressed his forehead against the windowpane" (299). This leads naturally into Kurlyandskaia's second observation: many of the verbs that Turgenev uses to describe behavior and reactions indicate external reflections of inner emotions.[2] Nikolay sighs (195), blushes (204), wipes his brow (204). Odintsova lowers her voice (289), bites the corner of her handkerchief (290), frowns (292). These are but a few examples of a phenomenon occurring on every page of *Fathers and Sons.* Here, in connection with surface information, we confront the question of Turgenev's use of psychological analysis, or as some critics maintain, his avoidance of it.

Most commentators argue that Turgenev's is a superficial psychology. Mazon, for instance, writes of the weakness of Turgenev's psychological portrayal:

> The author is satisfied with catching these [psychological] motifs in their external manifestations, in the acts of the heroes, in their words and gestures. He does not attempt to penetrate beyond the surface of phenomena.[3]

Matlaw writes in a similar vein:

> At his best, Turgenev transmits character without really indicating its formation or progress . . . . He never attempts to find the motivation behind his characters . . . he is concerned exclusively with surface phenomena.[4]

These statements are exaggerations—it is hardly the case that Turgenev *never* attempts to suggest motivation. And yet one must admit that Turgenev's psychology is primarily of the surface variety, but to criticize him for that is the equivalent of reproaching Brahms' orchestration for its lack of Mozartean lightness. Turgenev expounded very specific views on psychology and its uses in literature, and he practiced what he preached. He was opposed to what he conisdered excessive psycho-motivational detail. In a letter to L. Ya. Stechkina, a budding writer, he gave the following advice:

> Don't go into *excessive* detail about motivation . . .—a sensitive reader will believe you and understand you. (12_1, 359)

And:

> I don't know whether you've read a lot of Lev Tolstoy, but I'm certain that for you the study of that undoubtedly foremost Russian writer is positively harmful . . . . Every time that you touch upon nature, the results are splendid, all the more splendid because you use only two ot three strokes—but *characteristic* ones . . . And one must act in the same way in psychological work...*car le secret d'ennuyer est celui de tout dire.* (12_1, 317-318)

Turgenev's surface psychology is an integral part of his general novelistic technique, which is, improbably enough, cinematic at heart. *Fathers and Sons,* in particular, seems almost to have been written for the screen. Character in the novel is developed through individual scenes. As Matlaw points out, *Fathers and Sons* is a novel

> illustrating that the only requirement for Turgenev's purpose is a series of scenes each of which reveals character in a different way, illuminates it from a different angle or perspective, or demonstrates still another facet of its personality.[5]

Batyuto goes so far as to call these individual scenes "frames," and with good reason.[6] They follow each other in lightning succession, often without any transition. More importantly, and something that Batyuto does not remark, the frames often are arranged so as to create a montage effect, by virtue of which each frame acquires additional meaning because of its juxtaposition to preceding and succeeding ones. (Here we are in fact dealing with one of Eisenstein's most influential film discoveries.[7]) Consider, for instance, the conclusion of Chapter IV, where Pavel sits alone in his room late at night and muses:

> God knows where his thoughts wandered: the expression on his face was concentrated and gloomy, which does not occur when a person is occupied exclusively with reminiscences. (211)

The very next sentence, without even a paragraph break, describes Fenechka sitting in her room, her gaze directed at her baby's bed. The juxtaposition of these two scenes suggests an indirect and troubled link between Pavel and Fenechka. Such a technique is possible only in the novel or on the screen: it would be impossible on the stage, where transitions from one scene to another can never be quite instantaneous. Furthermore, Turgenev's descriptions of facial expressions are the equivalent of the cinematic close up. In general, Turgenev tends to show in his novels just what we might see on the screen. If Dostoevsky is an eminently dramatic novelist,[8] Turgenev may be properly called a cinematic novelist. All this may seem far removed from a discussion of Turgenev's psychology, but the point is that although Turgenev limits himself largely to surface reflections of a character's inner life (precisely what we would see on a screen), it does not follow that his use of psychology cannot be sophisticated or revealing. Consider Bazarov's leaning his feverish brow against the window pane (209), Fenechka's rushing into Nikolay's arms after Pavel has accused her of not loving her benefactor (361), or Katya's bemused raising of her eyes when Bazarov proclaims that individuals differ from each other no more than does one tree in a forest from another (277). Such quick external details are infinitely telling. Turgenev ought not to be faulted for his general extrinsic approach to psychological portaiture: it has yet to be demonstrated that anyone—writer, psychologist, or bio-chemist—can explain or describe adequately the workings of the human mind. Turgenev is well aware of the X-factor in human behavior, and he chooses not to describe the indescribable.

All this should not be taken to mean that Turgnev completely avoids analysis of motivations and thoughts. As noted earlier, one of the varieties of information relayed by protagonists and the narrator is that of evaluative remarks about behavior. Within the category of such evaluative information we find two major subdivisions: (1) characters' reactions to each other—including the narrator's reactions—and (2) explanations of characters' behavior and thoughts. As a general principle Turgenev has a character evaluate any other character with whom he comes into contact. This principle applies not only to the hero, but to all the major and many of the minor figures. In a certain sense it can be said that gossip is one of the major sources of information about personality and persons: Arkady and Bazarov discuss Pavel; Pavel discusses Bazarov and Arkady; and so on. Moreover, what any given character says of another tends to characterize the discussant more than the discussed. Since Bazarov and Arkady are exposed to more people in *Fathers and Sons* that any of the other players, it is natural that they should be the subjects of the greatest number of evaluative remarks and the stimulus for the majority of reactions. But of the two friends, Bazarov excites more comment: to reinforce this impression, Turgenev twice provides entire catalogues of reactions by a large group of characters to Bazarov (237, 358).

The narrator supplies us with two basic types of information about characters' thoughts and motivations: definitive and qualified analyses. In some cases he waxes omniscient, telling us precisely what is transpiring inside a person's mind. An example of this is the lengthy description of Bazarov's inner struggle with "romanticism" (285-287). Elsewhere the narrator only seems to guess at a given individual's motivations or thoughts; note, for instance, the narrator's multiple conjectures about what Nikolay may be thinking and feeling when Arkady runs off to introduce himself to Fenechka (214). In many of the qualified descriptions Russian words meaning "as if" *(slovno, budto, kak budto)* abound. In general the narration in *Fathers and Sons* is inconsistent: the narrator wavers between authorial omniscience and the limited first-person point of view of a faceless participant in the novel. One might argue that there are two narrative *personae* in *Fathers and Sons:* one an author-narrator who clearly stands above the work as its creator and who even occasionally addresses his reader directly— as a reader *(chitatel)* (195, 221), and another who seems to be an unidentifiable, passive participant in and witness to the events he describes. Note, for instance, the narrator's impressions of Kukshina:

> She spoke and moved very easily and at the same time awkwardly: she obviously considered herself an affable and simple creature, yet no matter what she did, it seemed to you that it was exactly what she had not wanted to do. (259)

Here the narrator seems to be on a par with Arkady and Bazarov rather than above them, creating them and the scene. This narrator describes surface phenomena; the other narrator indulges in motivational analysis. In short, Turgenev's narration is not as "objective" as some critics would have us believe: it occasionally calls attention to itself. Consider, for instance, Chapter VII, which Arkady narrates to Bazarov, although in fact we hear it from the narrator: "And Arkady told him his uncle's story. The reader will find it in the next chapter" (221). Most of the next chapter is clearly *not* narrated by the naive, inarticulate Arkady, who takes over the narration at the phrase " 'And so you see, Evgeny,' said Arkady, finishing up his story, 'how unjustly you judge Uncle!' " (225).

The discussion of Turgenev's narration has digressed somewhat from the major topic, Turgenev's use of psychological analysis in characterization. It was noted that Turgenev's restraint in the probing of the dialectics of the soul is perhaps a function of his awareness that man's behavior is irrational and ultimately impenetrable. At the same time, however, we should note that many of Turgenev's analyses suggest that for Turgenev man is a creature whose individual behavior is rarely *sui generis.* Fisher argues that Turgenev's psychology is not individual, as in Dostoevsky, but through the use of aphorisms is always anchored to a general law.[9] Exaggerated as the opinion may be, it contains a measure of truth. Individuals in *Fathers and Sons* are perceived as representatives of groups of characters, and in that connection Turgenev resorts to generalizations often in *Fathers and Sons*—thirty-two times, by my count.[10] Many of them begin with the word "as" *(kak)*, and are thus part of Turgenev's general reliance on simile for his imagery. Broadly speaking, the generalizations show a character's thoughts or actions to be in some way typical of a large group of people— children, women, humanity as a whole. They are not applied to everyone in equal proportions, however. An examination of this inequity is revealing. The following list indicates the number of times that psychological aphorisms are evoked to characterize the various *dramatis personae* in *Fathers and Sons:*

Arkady	8
Bazarov	2
Pavel	4
Nikolay	1
Odintsova	4
Kukshina	2
Fenechka	3
Katya	2

Of particular interest here is the contrast between the number of generalizations applied to Arkady and Bazarov, since they are the two characters to whom the greatest amount of space is devoted in the novel. Some characters, such as Bazarov, are clearly meant to appear more individual and less typical than others, and Arkady is not among them. (The alert reader will no doubt observe that Nikolay is the subject of the least number of generalizations in the novel. In his case, however, the fact that only one generalization is applied to him is a function not of his uniqueness, but of the fact that we see relatively little of him in the novel. We see Bazarov often, yet only twice is he characterized by generalizations.) It should be pointed out that the extensive use of generalizations is entirely appropriate in *Fathers and Sons,* one of whose themes is that children tend to become not unlike their parents (Arkady becomes a gentleman "farmer," Bazarov is a provincial doctor when we last see him), and that all humans are subject to the rule of fate.

The third category of information about characters—details relating to heredity and environment—is also a function of Turgenev's psychological technique. An individual's pre-history, as Reeve observes, is meant to reveal his character.[11] Matlaw argues that Turgenev does not manage to show the formation of personality, that he only reveals it,[12] but in the case of Pavel's pre-history, Matlaw would seem to overstate the case. Pavel's personality is reshaped by his encounter with Princess R., and we observe that transformation, or perhaps we should say deformation. Every major protagonist, with the crucial exception of Bazarov, has a pre-history of some sort, but some are more detailed than others. The particulars of Fenechka's and Katya's past, for instance, are skimpy: this dearth of detail may well be a reflection of what Fisher calls Turgenev's tendency "to ignore the psychology of types that are essentially alien to him."[13]

Especially important for characterization through environment is a character's choice of surroundings. Pavel's elegantly appointed room is an aspect of his person, as is Bazarov's father's cozily cluttered home. Similar environmental details are provided for Odintsova, Kukshina, and Fenechka, while Bazarov lacks any environment that is distinctly his own, and this very lack of a personalized setting is significant.[14]

All the types of information discussed so far may be related either directly by the narrator or by one or another of the persons in the novel. Most of the time it is the narrator himself who purveys information (except in the case of dialogue, of course), although Turgenev does occasionally narrate scenes or parts of them from the point of view of one of the participants. This type of indirect narration is largely restricted to Arkady. In many of the scenes in which he is present he is our observer. It is largely through his eyes that we see the land surrounding Marino (205); Pavel's pre-history, though not narrated by Arkady himself, is ostensibly from his point of view (Chapter VII); it is from Arkady's vantage point that we first observe Odintsova (265-267); much of the scene in Odintsova's hotel room is reported from Arkady's perspective, and many of the scenes between Arkady and Katya are told substantially from his point of view. Our initial perceptions of Bazarov are filtered through Arkady's eyes. Turgenev relies on Arkady because he is the most naive of the major characters. (Bazarov is perhaps more naive in a certain sense, but to use him as a point of view would render him less enigmatic.)

The second broad category of sources of information includes dialogue and monologue. Dialogue, as we shall see, plays a major role in the novel. It is there largely for purposes of characterization, rarely advancing the plot *per se* or serving for real communication among the characters. Instead, it allows the various protagonists to express their worldviews. The language in which each character speaks is a function of his worldview: the speech of each person is individualized. And just as important as words are silences. Batyuto points out:

> The text of a Turgenev novel literally teems with pauses and silences. The device of a long pause or silence, behind which, as a rule, is hidden a stream of thoughts, feelings, and emotions not always even named, but comprehensible to the sensitive reader, is a favorite means of psychological characterization that Turgenev uses generously.[15]

Until now the focus has been on the types of information that shape our perceptions of the protagonists in *Fathers and Sons*. At this point let us move on to an allied topic—the principle according to which information about characters is relayed. The major principle involved in characterization in *Fathers and Sons* is the exposition of such information as will most emphasize contrasts and parallels between and among characters and groups of characters.[16] It is here that we discover the answer to the second part of the question that Turgenev addressed to Fet: "And where are these pairs, believing and unbelieving?" (4, 371).

Almost everything in *Fathers and Sons* comes in pairs, and often the pairs are doubled. If we take the major characters as we are first introduced to them, they seem to pair off naturally according to age, locus, or blood or conjugal ties: Pavel and Nikolay —the older generation, men of the 1840s, brothers living together at Marino; Arkady and Bazarov—the new generation, men of the 1860s, university friends travelling together; Katya and Odintsova— sisters living together at Nikolskoe; Bazarov's parents—the older generation, socially inferior to the Kirsanovs; and Sitnikov and Kukshina—parodies of the new people. Such a grouping reflects the novel's alleged theme—the conflict between the generations— but it is entirely superficial. As Joel Blair notes, "the grouping of characters [in *Fathers and Sons*] that is the most obvious is not the most important."[17] Unless we move beyond this superficial pairing, we cannot hope to understand what *Fathers and Sons* is really about.

Of more substance is a grouping based on personality. If we identify those characters who are closest to each other in temperament and experience, we arrive at the following breakdown: Bazarov and Pavel; Arkady and Nikolay; and Odintsova and Bazarov/Pavel. Such a distribution is exactly what Blair has in mind when he writes:

> Our understanding of the novel develops as we observe the initial groups of characters dissolve and perceive the formation of new pairs. Eventually, those characters who seemed most unalike are aligned; their similarities become more important than their initial differences.[18]

That Bazarov and Pavel have much in common is a fact often overlooked until recently.[19] A cliché of Turgenev criticism holds that Pavel and Bazarov embody the conflicts between the men of the 1840s and the 1860s. That is of course true, but socio-political questions form only one strand in the novel's fabric—a strand whose significance is often exaggerated. Ralph Matlaw observes:

> [*Fathers and Sons*] is a novel illustrating that the only requirement for Turgenev's purposes is a series of scenes each of which reveals character in a different way, illuminates it from a different angle or

perspective, or demonstrates still another facet of its personality. The sociological or political aspects of the novels, which must necessarily be expressed in terms of plot rather than action [action for Matlaw means revelation of character], may be therefore shown as even less germane to the novels than it at first appears to be.[20]

The conflicts in the novel are the results of differences or similarities in temperament, with political ideology relegated to an inferior role. Failure to understand the real source of the conflicts in *Fathers and Sons* has led critics to overlook an essential similarity in temperament and experience between Bazarov and Pavel, the novel's primary ideological opponents.

Nikolay, when first introduced to Bazarov, firmly grasps his hand, "which the latter did not immediately offer" (200). When Pavel is introduced to Bazarov two chapters later, Pavel refuses to offer his hand; in fact, he puts it back in his pocket (208).[21] This is a minor moment, but a telling one. In this case the parallel underlines a trait Pavel and Bazarov share: haughtiness, not to say vanity, growing out of excessive pride. As Boyd points out, in Pavel we find the vanity of the aristocrat, in Bazarov that of the rebel.[22] Pavel's aristocratic vanity is emphasized by his fastidious attention to details of dress and toilette. In addition, in one of his verbal duels with Bazarov, Pavel announces: "It is precisely because of the sense of personal dignity that Mister—Mister Doctor so mocks that I shall not forget myself" (244). A few pages earlier the narrator tells us:

> On the other hand Pavel Petrovich hated Bazarov with all the strength of this soul: he considered him a monster of pride, an impudent fellow, a cynic and plebeian; he suspected that Bazarov did not respect him— him, Pavel Kirsanov! (237)

Bazarov is no less proud. When Arkady asks him whether he holds a high opinion of himself, Bazarov responds: "When I meet a person who doesn't give in to me . . . then I'll change my opinion about myself" (325). Moreover, when Bazarov declares that he needs people like Sitnikov because "Really, it's not for the gods to glaze pottery," Arkady at long last perceives "the bottomless abyss of Bazarov's egoism" (304).

Pavel's and Bazarov's peculiar debating style is a function of their pride and self-absorption. Both are stubborn and set in their opinions; neither is really interested in what anyone else has to say. They do not analyze their own or each other's views. S. M. Petrov suggest that they do not really argue—they are articulating their positions.²³ Their dialogues are largely monologues that run parallel to each other.

Neither Bazarov nor Pavel readily capitulates in the face of opposition. While Nikolay is ready to accept the younger generation's sweeping dismissal of him and his generation, Pavel objects: "Well, I won't surrender so quickly . . . That doctor and I are going to have it out, I can feel it coming" (240). Bazarov, in his farewell to Arkady, says accusingly: "You, for example, won't fight— and imagine yourselves heroes, but we want to fight" (380).

Pavel and Bazarov display similar tactics in analogous situations. Bazarov is tactiturn around Nikolay and Pavel: "As a rule, Bazarov spoke little in the presence of the 'old Kirsanovs' . . ." (240-241). When he does occasionally break his silence, he tends to do so in rude, abrupt, niggardly monosyllables. Pavel's behavior among people whom he views as the older generation is strikingly similar. In Chapter VII we learn that he "left the estate only for elections, where for the main part he was silent, only occasionally irritating and frightening the landowners of the older generation with his liberal sallies . . ." (225). Clearly Bazarov and Pavel both know the value of shock effect, though Bazarov is more skilled in its application. As Moser says:

> Since neither [Bazarov nor Pavel] is genuinely willing to listen to the other, no meeting of minds occurs, but Bazarov usually bests his opponent because he is quite willing to push his arguments to their logical extreme upon provocation, whereupon Pavel Petrovich can only gape.²⁴

The most vivid example of their similarly militant pride remains, of course, the duel.

Pavel and Bazarov both undergo radical personality changes as a result of confrontations with "fatal" women. Pavel's prehistory, related in the inserted novella *(vstavnaia novella)* which comprises most of Chapter VII, serves as an ironic foreshadowing of Bazarov's experiences with Odintsova. Reducing Chapter VII to its relevant essentials, we recall that Pavel, a frivolous young nobleman, plays the rake and enchants everyone with his manner, which is "self-assured, faintly ironical, and somehow amusingly caustic"

(221). A brilliant career awaits him, but his prospects of success are altered drastically by his encounter with the Princess R., with whom he promptly falls in love after meeting her at a ball. Pavel, "accustomed to easy conquests" (222), quickly achieves his desired ends, but he is amazed to discover that his ardor fails to cool. He pursues the Princess R., who is alternately in and out of love with him, all over Europe. Their affair ends in Baden: "Within a month it was all over: the fire flared up for the last time and went out forever" (223). Pavel returns to Russia a changed man. He eventually retires to his brother's estate, where he looks after his personal toilette, rarely goes out into society, and leads a solitary, joyless existence. An unrequited love has destroyed him.

Bazarov can only mock Pavel's tragedy:

> All the same, I hold that a man who has staked his whole life on the card of a woman's love, and then, when he has lost, turns sour and allows himself to drift—a creature like that is not a man, but just a male animal. (226)

Irrational, passionate love is nonsense to Bazarov: "And what are these mysterious relations between men and women? We physiologists know what these relations are" (226). But, in perhaps the most striking instance of analogy in the novel, Bazarov's confrontation with Odintsova and the irrational repeats the main outlines of Pavel's pre-history.

Like Pavel, Bazarov displays a self-assured, ironical, caustic manner, though unlike Pavel, he does not precisely enchant everyone. Like Pavel, he is a man of whom others entertain great expectations. Arkady tells Bazarov's father, for instance: "I am certain . . . that a great future awaits your son, that he will do honor to your name" (319). Odintsova also senses Bazarov's enormous potential (297), and on his death bed Bazarov himself admits that he had thought of himself as a giant *(gigant)* (396). But Bazarov's potentially great career is cut short by his experience with Odintsova, whom, significantly, he first meets at a ball, just as Pavel had met Princess R. at a ball. There is sufficient textual evidence to assume that up to his meeting with Odintsova Bazarov's relations with women had been not unlike Pavel's:

> Bazarov was a great admirer of women and female beauty, but love in the ideal, or as he expressed it, romantic sense, he called lunacy, un-

pardonable idiocy . . . "If you like a certain woman," he would say, "try to get what you want; and if you can't—well, so what, drop her—there are other women." (286-287)

And, though he fails to "get what he wants *(dobitsia tolku),*" he finds, as had been Pavel's experience with Princess R., that he lacks the resolution to drop Odintsova (287). Instead, even after his humiliating rejection by her ("You have misunderstood me" [299] she whispers), Bazarov, not unlike Pavel in his pursuit of the Princess R. through Europe, makes two final, hopeless returns to Odintsova's estate. After that he, like Pavel, returns to the family estate to lick his wounds and brood. As Bazarov is dying he asks that Odintsova come to see him, and his last words are saturated with romantic pathos: "Blow out the dying lamp, and let it go out . . . Enough! . . . Now . . . darkness . . ." (396). The imagery is a visual echo of the dying fire imagery surrounding Pavel's last encounter with Princess R. in Baden.

Neither Pavel nor Bazarov is open to esthetic pleasure. In Chapter XI the narrator describes Nikolay's pleasantly melancholy meditations as he looks at the stars of a summer sky. Pavel's emotions are then contrasted:

> Pavel Petrovich reached the end of the garden, and he also sank into meditation, and also raised his eyes to the heavens. But there was nothing reflected in his beautiful dark eyes except the light of the stars. He was not born a romantic . . . . (252)[25]

In an analogous scene at Bazarov's parents' estate, Vasily, coming across Bazarov and Arkady lying in the hay, remarks: "Lying on the 'earth,' looking at the 'sky'... You know—there's a special meaning to that." Bazarov cuts him off: "I only look at the sky when I want to sneeze" (327). This instance of scenic parallelism serves to underline an indifference to the wonder, mystery, and beauty of nature—an indifference that Pavel and Bazarov have in common. An additional demonstration of Bazarov's lack of awe before nature is his too-often-quoted "Nature is not a temple, but a workshop" (236). Finally, the narrator at one point states explicitly that Bazarov is essentially indifferent to the beauties of nature (286).

That Pavel is not especially attracted to art is everywhere apparent: in his youth he read but five or six French novels (221).

In his arguments with Bazarov he specifically mentions that it is his brother Nikolay who is so taken with German poetry (219).[26] His beautifully appointed room is more likely a reflection of his social status and Anglomania than of any particular esthetic sensibilities. Bazarov is not merely uninterested in art: his utilitarian principles make him denigrate its value. "A decent chemist is twenty times more useful than any poet" (219), he proclaims in one of his more militant (and clichéd) moments. In a less martial mood he admits to Odintsova that he has no feeling for art (276), at the same time wondering why anyone needs such feelings (277).[27]

Another significant similarity between Pavel and Bazarov centers around Fenechka. Blair suggests that "the qualities revealed by the interviews of Bazarov and Pavel with Fenechka are identical: naturalness, tenderness, attention to and admiration of a young mother and her child."[28] But there is more involved here than admiration for a young mother and her child. Pavel and Bazarov are both strongly attracted to Fenechka, but for different reasons. What does link their common attraction to Fenechka is the fact that their interest in her is not disinterested. Neither is drawn to Fenechka by charms that are uniquely her own. Pavel and Bazarov see in her not a person in her own right, but an image (in Bazarov's case, a reverse image) of a lost love. Since Fenechka reminds Pavel of Princess R., his affection for her is tinged with melancholy recollections and guilt: she is after all his brother's mistress. For Bazarov Fenechka is everything that Odintsova is not. Bazarov's flirtation with Fenechka strikes us as very unusual behavior on his part. Their interviews, especially the ones in the garden (Ch. XXIII), with its motifs of nervous giggles, teaching a peasant girl to read, and exchanging flowers for kisses, read like a parody of Pushkin's "Mistress into Maid" *(Baryshnya-krestianka)* —in itself a parody. The Bazarov we see in the garden with Fenechka strikes us as radically unlike the Bazarov whom we see anywhere else in the novel: his tone is light, bantering, coquettish. One critic has called him "almost *poshly*" in this scene.[29] We can easily discern the reason for Bazarov's behavior: he is play-acting. Having recently been wounded to the quick by his all-too-real confrontation with Odintsova, he seeks refuge in a flirtation which is essentially meaningless and which he knows can never lead anywhere: he cannot be hurt personally by it. Bazarov manipulates Fenechka for his own purposes, and the insensitivity he displays toward her and her position in the Kirsanov household makes this a scene in which Bazarov appears considerably less than ingratiating.[30]

Even in their disagreements, Pavel and Bazarov display similar attitudes. They argue about the virtues of the Russian *narod*,[31] but in fact both are profoundly contemptuous of the peasantry. Pavel sniffs eau de cologne when he speaks to them (226), and Bazarov hates "Filip and Sidor," to whose betterment he is supposed to devote himself (325). The sources of their contempt are different. As Boyd points out: "Pavel Petrovich's contempt is that of a master for his slaves, while Bazarov is exasperated by their indolence and apathy."[32] But the end results are the same: by the close of the novel the peasants call Bazarov a gentleman *(barin)*, thus putting him, as far as they are concerned, in the same camp with Pavel (384).[33]

A final minor but amusing instance of parallelism between Bazarov and Pavel involves card playing. Pavel is admired in the neighborhood because he "plays whist in a masterly fashion and always loses" (225). Bazarov plays whist twice in the course of the novel, once with Odintsova and Porfiry Platonych (Ch. XVI) and once with his father and the priest (XXI): he loses consistently.[34]

If Bazarov and Pavel are so alike in their pride, exclusion from the world of esthetic pleasure, and lack of a rewarding inner life (except vis-à-vis their love lives), why are they the opponents in the novel? One answer is that they are nonetheless ideologically opposed to each other, although their respective ideologies are anything but cohesive and coherent. A more substantial answer, however, draws on the fundamental laws of magnetism: likes repel. We can see how the axiom is corroborated in the novel if we recall that Pavel and Bazarov accuse each other of the same thing— limitless and unfounded vanity.

That Bazarov and Pavel loathe each other because of similar personality traits was observed early by Pisarev:

> Pavel . . . is an obsolete shadow of the Pechorin type . . . . Pechorin and Bazarov types hate and repel each other. Pechorins and Bazarovs absolutely cannot exist together in the same society because both Pechorins and Bazarovs are made of the same material . . . Pechorins and Bazarovs are completely dissimilar in regard to their activities; but they are absolutely alike in the typical characteristics of their personalities. . . .[35]

Finally, is it not likely that Bazarov and Pavel are the "unbelieving" pair of which Fet wrote to Turgenev? One suspects that they are, and that Fet meant the word not specifically in a religious sense, but in the sense that Bazarov and Pavel do not have faith in anything or anyone except themselves. They are not open to the traditional non-religious sources of human inspiration—love, nature, art.

It is also possible that Fet had Bazarov and Odintsova in mind when he spoke of "believing and unbelieving pairs." Odintsova has certain traits that link her to Pavel, others that link her to Pavel *and* Bazarov, and these three characters form one of the three "camps" within the novel.

Some scholars have tried to show parallels between Odintsova and Princess R. Byaly, for instance, argues that the characterization of both heroines is based on antitheses and mystery.[36] In this way, he reasons, "Turgenev confronts his Bazarov with the real existence of what had been for him no more than a fiction, 'romanticism, nonsense, rot, art.'"[37] Similarly, Blair argues that Odintsova is "a realistic version of the melodramatic caricature of Princess R."[38] This is to confuse structural and stylistic parallels, however, with insubstantial similarities of character. Odintsova and Princess R. play analogous roles in the lives of Bazarov and Pavel, but they have little in common as personality types. Batyuto asks: "In point of fact, is there much in common between the calm and well-balanced, 'clear as daylight' genteel-epicurean Odintsova and the tortured, mysterious, at times almost mad Princess R.?"[39] Their temperaments are as different as night and day. We cannot deny that Odintsova at times displays the frantic, hysterical tendencies that are typical of Princess R., who is flighty during the day and racked by anguish at night (222). Odintsova paces nervously around her room after Bazarov's confession (299), but the point is that such behavior is unusual for her; her calm is rarely shattered for any length of time, while Princess R. is manic-depressive by nature.

It should be noted that oblique, "hereditary" links between Princess R. and Odintsova can be established by going outside the novel in search of prototypes. Batyuto, for instance, links Princess R. to the heroine of "A Correspondence": both heroines enslave the men who love them.[40] Then, by appealing to Kiyko's work on "A Correspondence," Batyuto goes on to suggest Pauline Viardot as a prototype for both Princess R. and Odintsova. But one may with equal justification posit Mariya Alexandrovna, the heroine of "A Correspondence," as a forerunner of Odintsova: like Odintsova, she is an emancipated woman of sorts who lives in the country with her sister. She refuses the roles traditionally assigned a woman by bourgeois society—wife, mother, housemaker—and the neighbors think of her as a wild woman. So we may conclude that although Princess R. and Odintsova play similar structural roles in *Fathers and Sons,* and although they share a common prototype, their natures are very different. The characters in the novel to whom Odintsova is closest in temperament are Pavel and Bazarov.

Odintsova shares with Pavel an attachment to order and superficial stability. The neighbors respect Pavel for the fact that even though he has retired to the provinces, he has not let himself go to seed. His dress and conduct continue to be impeccable. Similarly, Odintsova pays considerable attention to dress and scheduling. Life at Nikolskoe follows a preordained pattern. When Bazarov objects to this rigidity, Odintsova defends herself by saying:

> You are right from your point of view—and perhaps, in this case, I am the genteel noblewoman; but one cannot live in the country without order; boredom would overtake one. (285)

In addition, the imagery surrounding Pavel and Odintsova underscores the fact that they are both spiritually dead. Odintsova sleeps "all pure and frigid in her clean and fragrant linen" (284). In the Paris manuscript we find Odintsova "pure as marble" (456/271). A few lines later there is a description of her motionless sleep (456/272). The emphasis is clear: Odintsova is calm and cold —a corpse. The portrait of Pavel recuperating after the duel employs similar imagery:

> Pavel Petrovich moistened his forehead with eau-de-cologne and closed his eyes. His handsome, wasted head, illuminated by the brilliant daylight, lay on the white pillow like the head of a corpse... Indeed, he was a corpse. (363)

Odintsova shares with Pavel and Bazarov an indifference to nature, music, and the arts in general. The narrator points out, for instance, that she *and* Bazarov are immune to the charms of nature (286). It is Katya who plays the piano while Odintsova plays whist with Bazarov—the card playing yet another motif linking Pavel,

Bazarov, and Odintsova. Furthermore, like the two men, Odintsova is endowed with strength of will and an overriding concern for spiritual freedom. As she thinks about the affair with Bazarov that might have been, she concludes: "No... God knows where it might have led, it's nothing to be joked with, peace *(spokoystvie)* is still better than anything on earth" (300). Similarly, Bazarov tells Arkady:

> If you don't quite understand me, then I'll tell you the following: in my opinion, it's better to break stones on the roadway than to allow a woman to possess so much as the tip of your finger. (306)

Bazarov, Pavel, and Odintsova all belong to the camp of the strong, the egoistic, and the sterile. There are, of course, differences among the three. Whereas Pavel's and Odintsova's coldness and indifference are thoroughgoing and genuine, Bazarov's are untested, and once they are challenged, they prove eminently assailable. His strong will and egoism, however, are constants in his personality, and they ally him with Pavel and Odintsova. All these characters impress us with their strength. We are not shown its sources, but the emanations of that psychic energy are everywhere discernible. These characters all have the power to influence other people: Bazarov is the novel's most influential protagonist, but Odintsova has Katya and Bazarov under her thumb through some of the novel, and Nikolay and Fenechka live in dread of Pavel's censure. These strong individuals react intensely—even violently—to the other protagonists in their own camp. Pavel and Bazarov fight a duel. Bazarov embraces Odintsova like a wild animal, or so it seems to her (300). All the members of this group are egoists, as a result of which they are the observed, rather than observers within the novel. In formal terms this means that individual scenes are hardly ever narrated from their point of view. Their self-preoccupation does not permit genuine interest in anyone or anything outside of themselves.

The group of strong, sterile egoists—the unbelievers—is contrasted to a second major group, which is composed of characters who are meek, altruistic, and fertile.[41] Like the strong group, it comprises pairs of characters who display similar termperaments and interests.

Arkady and Nikolay are close to each other in temperament, and as character types they are contrasted with Pavel and Bazarov.

One ought not forget that the novel's title links the generations just as much as and perhaps more than it contrasts them. One of the novel's major themes, as mentioned earlier, is that it is the children's fate to become like their fathers. That theme is emphasized by the relations between Arkady and Nikolay. Arkady, for all his desire to be like Bazarov, is not: he is his father's son. Their resemblance is underscored in a number of ways. Both father and son are raised at home in the provinces. Both are taken by their fathers to St. Petersburg to enroll in the university. Both receive their degrees, retire to the family estate with their wives, and occupy themselves with managing the estate. These parallels are first sounded in the opening chapter, when we are introduced to Nikolay: "And so we meet him [Nikolay], in the month of May, 1859 . . . waiting for the arrival of his son who, as he himself had once done, had just taken his degree" (198).

Arkady and Nikolay pay lip service to the fashionable intellectual trends of the day. Arkady fancies himself a nihilist and spouts one prepared nihilist maxim after another: "I have already told you, Uncle, that we recognize no authorities" (243), he declares to Pavel. Nikolay, like Arkady, feigns interest in current ideas. He tells Bazarov:

> For my part, I'm very glad that you're studying the natural sciences. I've heard that Liebig has made amazing discoveries in connection with the fertilization of fields. You can help me in my agronomical work: you can give me some useful advice. (220)

All Arkady and Nikolay's remarks about contemporary trends ring false: they sound prepared, bookish. Father and son's real commitments are to music, art, poetry, nature, and the life of the emotions. In Chapter XI Nikolay sits alone in the garden musing on Bazarov's rejection of nature: " 'But to reject poetry?' he asked himself again. 'To lack any feeling for art, nature...' " (249). He surveys the landscape: " 'How beautiful, O Lord!' thought Nikolay Petrovich, and some favorite lines of verse came to his lips" (250). There are at least two similar scenes involving Arkady. In Chapter III Arkady first perceives the landscape through Bazarov's eyes, as it were, and comes to the conclusion that there is no prosperity on his native estate and that it must be transformed. "Such were Arkady's reflections... While he meditated, spring claimed its own *(vziala svoe)*" (205). Thereupon follows another typically Turgenevian lyrical description of the same landscape. "Arkady stared and stared, and his thoughts gradually growing weaker, disappeared..." (206). In a much later chapter Arkady questions Bazarov about nature. " 'And is nature nonsense?' Arkady asked, gazing thoughtfully at the far-flung, variegated fields, illuminated by the beautiful mellow light of the setting sun" (236). Incidentally, in the Paris manuscript Arkady's love of nature is made explicit very early in the novel (448/206). Perhaps Turgenev removed the passage that emphasizes Arkady's involuntary passionate response to nature so as not to give away Arkady's pseudo-nihilism too soon.

Arkady and Nikolay's love of music is likewise stressed. Nikolay plays Schubert's "Erwartung" on his cello in the moonlight (236); Arkady is moved by Katya's performance of Mozart's "Sonata Fantasia in C Minor" (281). What Turgenev is pointing out here, of course, is that Arkady and his father have rewarding inner lives and that they are committed to something outside themselves.

Pushkin's poetry provides another link between father and son. In Chapter III Nikolay quotes *Eugene Onegin* to Arkady; and in Chapter X Arkady, at Bazarov's urging, takes Pushkin's "The Gypsies" away from his father and offers Büchner's tome in its place (239). Yet Arkady is knowledgeable enough about Pushkin to recognize that Bazarov's Pushkin quotation in Chapter XXI is counterfeit. And he is fond enough of the poet to accuse Bazarov of slander when the latter inanely claims that Pushkin is a martial poet (325-326).

Arkady and Nikolay are both easily moved to tears. At the conclusion of Nikolay's pleasantly melancholy meditations in the garden, we find:

> Oh, how Bazarov would have laughed at him if he had found out what was going on inside him at that moment. Arkady himself would have criticized him. Here he was at forty-four, a gentleman farmer and landowner, shedding tears, inexplicable tears: that was a hundred times worse than the cello. (251)

In a much later scene Arkady, who still fancies himself in love with Odintsova, remarks that Bazarov has spent a long time with her that evening. Bazarov says yes, he was with Odintsova the whole time that Arkady was playing the piano with Katya. " 'I didn't play...' began Arkady and fell silent. He felt tears coming to his eyes but did not want to start crying in the presence of his mocking friend" (295). Arkady weeps in at least two other scenes in the novel (303, 381).

Father and son are charmingly inarticulate at moments when they are being sincere. (Therefore their articulateness about burning issues of the day strikes us as all the more suspicious.) Nikolay's confessions about his relationship with Fenechka (Ch. III) are blushingly tortured, and the preamble to Arkady's declaration of love to Katya is quite incomprehensible: "I assume it is the duty of every honest man to be completely frank with those... with those who... in a word, with those whom he holds dear, and so I... I intend..." (275-276). Another example of their parallel inarticulateness can be found in the epilogue, when neither father nor son is able to offer a properly rhetorical toast to the departing Pavel (398). Instead they abandon the idea of a toast and proceed directly to embraces, thus demonstrating their real commitment to the life of the heart rather than that of the mind.

The last parallel to be traced between Nikolay and Arkady is perhaps the most significant. It centers around their married lives. In the first chapter we find a description of Nikolay's first marriage:

> The couple lived well and tranquilly: they almost never parted from each other, they read together, played piano pieces for four hands, sang duets; she planted flowers and looked after the poultry yard, he occasionally hunted and managed the estate.... (198)

Arkady and Katya spend their time together in much the same way: they read, listen to music, and feel comfortable with each other—even when they are silent. The opening scene of Chapter XXV is particularly revealing. Katya and Arkady are seated in the garden at Nikolskoe:

> Arkady and Katya were both silent; he held in his hands a half-opened book, and she was picking out of the basket the crumbs of white bread remaining in it and throwing them to a small family of sparrows... They were both silent, but their very silence and the way they sat together spoke eloquently of their confiding intimacy; each seemed not to be thinking of the other, yet secretly felt joy at the other's proximity. (363-364)

Here we note that the parallels include not only the sense of calm and quiet intimacy, but even extend to the feeding of birds (cf. Nikolay's wife's managing the poultry yard).

In the Paris manuscript there are analogies drawn between Nikolay's initial attitude toward Fenechka and Arkady's toward Katya. In describing the history of Nikolay's acquaintance with Fenechka, the canonical text mentions Fenechka's mother, whom Nikolay hires as a housekeeper: "Her husband had died long ago, leaving her an only daughter, Fenechka" (232). The Paris manuscript goes on: "Fenechka, whom Nikolay Petrovich saw for the first time the next morning, but to whom he paid no attention at the time" (451). Arkady's first response to Katya is similar: he is so taken with Odintsova that he fails to find any special virtues in her younger sister (282).

In more general terms, Arkady and Nikolay are alike in that they are healthily and appealingly average men whose inner lives are warmed by an intense love of nature, music, poetry, and their wives and friends. It is interesting to note that Turgenev attributed to Arkady and Nikolay traits that were his own. In a letter of October 3, 1860, to E. E. Lambert, he writes: "I want to explain to you just why it is that my daughter and I have so little in common: she doesn't love either music, or poetry, or nature—or dogs, and those are the only things I do love" (4, 982).

Arkady and Nikolay may be limited, but they have a capacity for generosity and happiness. They interact with nature and the natural processes, unlike Bazarov and Pavel, who try to counteract or oppose them. It seems likely that Arkady and Nikolay are the "believing" pair of whom Fet wrote. Or perhaps he meant Katya and Arkady. Arkady, Nikolay, and Katya are all members of the group of "believers." This group—the meek, altruistic, and fertile—also includes Fenechka and Bazarov's parents. Those comprising this group have additional traits in common.

Arkady, Nikolay, Fenechka (and Sitnikov and Kukshina, in addition), are linked by timidity: the words "timidity, timid, to be timid" *(robost, robky, robet)* are used to describe all of these individuals. Bazarov's parents belong to this camp as well, though the word "timid" is not specifically applied to them. But note, for instance, that Bazarov's father does not dare to show his true feelings to his son (320), and Bazarov's mother is even afraid to touch him (330). This entire group is contrasted to Odintsova, Pavel, and

Bazarov—strong characters who value their independence and who, though subject to fear (Odintsova and Bazarov terrify each other), could hardly be accused of timidity. Katya occupies a middle position between the two groups. The narration makes this clear by emphasizing that Katya is *not* timid or shy *(robkaia)*: "She was not exactly shy *(ne to chto robkaia)*, but distrustful and a little frightened of her sister who had raised her and did not suspect it [her state of fright] " (281). There is more to Katya than is apparent at first glance, and we shall return to her later.

The characters in the "believing" group are observers rather than the observed. It was noted earlier that Arkady is often *our* observer in most of the scenes in which he is present. But there are other observers in the novel, Katya and Nikolay being the most prominent among them. When Bazarov and Arkady first arrive at Nikolskoe, Katya says little, but watches intently (277-278). Later in the novel Arkady notes that Katya is very observant (366). At the confrontations between Bazarov and Pavel, Nikolay, like his son, says very little. He hovers over the scene and watches. Another passive observer is Bazarov's mother, whose gaze is focused exclusively on her son (315, 330). She literally sees no one but him.

Certain parallels can be drawn between the fathers, Nikolay and Vasily. They are linked by a concern for form, especially in their relations with their sons. (It is generally true in the novel as a whole that the older generation is more concerned with form than is its younger counterpart.) Nikolay is painfully embarrassed by his liaison with Fenechka; Vasily hides the extent of his religiosity from his son (328), removes his beloved military decorations for the duration of his son's stay (330), is too afraid of Bazarov's censure to use a houseboy to drive away flies during the meals (315), and is beside himself when he discovers that Bazarov has learned that he ordered that a serf be flogged (332). Another aspect of this concern for form is the fathers' attempts to "keep up with the times." Nikolay complains that although he has set up a model farm and that he reads, studies, and generally does his utmost to stay abreast of contemporary developments, Bazarov and Arkady still conclude that "his song is already sung" (239). In the Paris manuscript, Vasily states unambiguously that he "tries not to fall behind the age" (312), and like Nikolay, he considers himself a "homo novus" (318), but Bazarov mocks his father for mentioning Rademacher and for having a copy of the journal *The Friend of Health* that is four years old (312). Another motif shared by the fathers is their love of meditation. Nikolay often abandons himself to sweetly melancholic revery (249-251); Vasily points out his favorite bench to Bazarov and Arkady: "On this spot I like to philosophize while watching the sunset" (316).

The members of the "believing" group are all distinguished by an absence of egoism. Within Turgenev's world it is precisely this element that allows them all to attach themselves to the world at large: it gives them the capacity to love, as a result of which they enjoy life. Their expectations are not great, and their lives are all the richer because of that. Like Tolstoy's and Dostoevsky's "average" heroes and heroines, they attempt neither to understand the world nor to change it, and this is their salvation and the source of their strength.

There is a third group of characters in *Fathers and Sons* that comprises various individuals (and animals) whose function within the novel is to double the major protagonists. These doublings are ironic in nature.

In the opening chapter Nikolay, awaiting the arrival of his son, examines the steps of the posting house: "A large, gaudy chicken was strutting along them, stamping firmly with large yellow legs; a filthy cat was eyeing him hostilely, sprawled affectedly on the bannister. The sun was blazing..." (198). Here in miniature is a foreshadowing of the drama about to be played out in the summer sun between the gaudy, self-important Pavel and the hostile, occasionally mud-bespattered Bazarov.[42]

In the same chapter we are introduced to Nikolay's valet, Peter, whom the narrator describes as "a representative of a modern and more perfect age" (195). When Arkady arrives, Peter, "who as a modernized servant, had not kissed the master's hand, merely bowed to him from a distance, then disappeared again beyond the gate" (200). Peter is contrasted to Prokofich, the old family servant who is immaculately tailored and something of an aristocrat in his own right. On seeing Arkady he grins and kisses his hand, but only bows to Bazarov (207). The generation conflict, then, is first visible in the servants. And, of course, the issue of kissing hands or not kissing them explicitly parallels Bazarov's and Pavel's offering or not offering their hands.

The last example of pairing among minor characters is Sitnikov and Kukshina. In the critical literature on *Fathers and*

Sons, they are usually identified as parodies of the "new people" of whom Bazarov is a genuine representative. This is fine as far as it goes, but it would be more accurate to describe Sitnikov as Bazarov's parodic double and Kukshina as Odintsova's. Sitnikov's half-baked nihilism and slavish devotion to Bazarov drive home for the reader the difference between a pseudo-nihilist and an authentic one. In addition, the presence of someone so blatantly absurd as Sitnikov makes less likely the possibility of the reader's perceiving Bazarov as a caricature.[43]

Kukshina and Odintsova are doubled in several ways. Both are young and husbandless; Kukshina is separated from her husband, while Odintsova is a young widow. Both manage their own estates and enjoy a reputation as emancipated women. Both pepper Bazarov with questions about the leading issues of the day. (Kukshina's questions are absurd, Odintsova's tactical.) Both are interested in chemistry: Kukshina has created a new mastic for dolls' heads (260), while Odintsova expects Bazarov to give her a few chemistry lessons (289). (In fact, of course, it is she who gives Bazarov some lessons in chemistry—or should we say bio-chemistry?) Kukshina and Odintsova are alike in their attitude to Bazarov. Kukshina tells Bazarov: "You perhaps don't know that I am terribly afraid of you. . . . You are a dangerous gentleman..." (260). Here Kukshina is babbling flirtatiously. Compare Odintsova's reaction when Bazarov embraces her: " 'You have misunderstood me,' she whispered hastily in fright. She looked as if she might scream if he took another step..." (299). At their meeting the next day, "I am afraid of this person" flashes through Odintsova's mind (301).

What can we say in conclusion about characterization in *Fathers and Sons?* It should be obvious by now that the parallels and contrasts implied in its title not only determine the compositional pattern of the novel, but are the basis of characterization as well. Information about characters is imparted in such a way that individuals are perceived as representatives of distinct groups, and in the contrasts among these groups are to be found the keys to the novel's interpretation. The most obvious groupings—the fathers and the sons—are the least substantial for understanding the novel as a work of imaginative literature. The truly significant groupings contrast the strong and the meek, the egoists and altruists, the sterile and the fruitful: and these groupings cut across the categories of generation, class, and political ideology. If we do not understand that, we will have missed the fundamental theme of the novel: the meek shall indeed inherit the earth, and they shall bring forth much fruit and multiply.

III

CHARACTERIZATION IN *FATHERS AND SONS*: INDIVIDUALS

In the preceding chapter the topic was the general methods of characterization in *Fathers and Sons* and the principles—parallels and contrast—according to which they are applied. This involved demonstrating that characters in the novel are perceived in pairs and that the pairs combine to form three groups of protagonists. In the present chapter we turn to the individual players and elaborate on matters of characterization that apply to them not as representatives of groups, but as individuals. It seems only logical to begin with the novel's most commanding figure, Bazarov.

Having read *Fathers and Sons* and masses of critical material, we may still ask ourselves the same questions that Odintsova addresses to Bazarov:

> Listen, I've long been wanting to clear up some things with you. There's no point in telling you—you yourself know it—that you are not an average person; you're still young—your whole life is still ahead of you. What are you preparing yourself for? What sort of future awaits you? I mean—what goal do you want to achieve, where are you going, what makes you tick? In a word, who are you, what are you? (297)

Her query is to the point: who is Bazarov? Few if any critics doubt his greatness, or at least his potential for greatness,[1] yet there have been few persuasive analyses of that greatness. Until recently many works dwelt on the notion that Bazarov is a budding revolutionary, which is synonymous with distinction, magnitude, power. Needless to say, this is not a very satisfactory explanation. Many critics have commented on Bazarov's strength, yet if by strength we mean will, then Pavel is nearly as strong, and Odintsova is far stronger. Pustovoit asserts that we are everywhere struck by the clarity and vigor of Bazarov's intellect as it reveals itself in verbal confrontations with Pavel.[2] But if we are honest, we must acknowledge that many of Bazarov's remarks sound fatuous and rather juvenile. The "nobility of Bazarov's character" is another trait passed around from critic to critic, yet what sort of nobility does our hero display in flirting irrresponsibly with Fenechka, in hurting his parents, and in revelling in his capacity for hatred?

Yet we remain convinced of Bazarov's stature, even though we cannot identify its sources. To a certain extent Bazarov's so-called greatness is a brilliant literary trick. At the conclusion of the novel Turgenev leaves us mourning the untimely loss of a great man whose merit is more an item of faith than fact.[3] So the question remains—why are we convinced?

Part of the answer lies in the fact that the other characters in the novel react strongly to Bazarov.[4] Arkady attempts to model himself on his friend, Pavel is irritated by Bazarov almost to the point of apoplexy, Sitnikov cowers and simpers before him, Odintsova is titillated and frightened by him, Katya thinks of him as a wild beast, Prokofich can scarcely tolerate his presence, Fenechka is enchanted by him, and Bazarov's parents dote on him. In other words, Bazarov is the major generator of emotional energy in the novel. People react to him in contradictory ways, but they all react—often violently. Thus we become convinced of Bazarov's strength of character because we see its emanations, not its sources.

Throughout much of the novel Bazarov is an enigmatic presence. His original status is that of the stranger, and to a large extent that status remains unchanged. We learn nothing of Bazarov's pre-history, except for what we can infer from his parents' way of life. A common motif in others' remarks about him and to him is a lack of comprehension. Arkady, Odintsova, Katya, Pavel, and Bazarov's father all say one or more times that they do not understand one or another of Bazarov's actions or assertions. And many of Bazarov's actions *are* inexplicable: why, for example, does he wait for so long to treat the cut which he knows can cause his death? Our answers necessarily fall into the category of speculation.[5]

We know as little about Bazarov's plans for the future as we do of his past. Whatever textual clues exist are contradictory. Bazarov informs the two peasant boys with whom he hunts frogs that he needs to study the frogs so that he will be able to treat the boys if they ever fall sick, and he tells Odintsova that he plans to become a country doctor (297). She does not believe him for a minute, and neither do we. We know from Turgenev's correspondence that he intended Bazarov as the portrait of a revolutionary,[6] but the textual evidence in the novel he wrote leaves us unconvinced.

Bazarov is plainly a character who promises much more than he offers, yet we respond to him with sympathy. Why? What features compensate for all the unfulfilled promises? There are several. Bazarov is a risk-taker who is willing to accept the consequences for his actions. No one else in the novel—with the exception of Pavel in his past life—exposes himself to perils that are at all significant. Arkady almost consistently fails to realize his desires in action, whether that means giving in to his love of nature, admitting himself to be under Bazarov's negative influence, or toasting Bazarov at Pavel's farewell dinner. His most memorable gamble is proposing to Katya—a proposal made nearly unavoidable by Odintsova's overheard remarks to Bazarov indicating that Arkady's interest in Katya is that of a brother. Nikolay will not hazard keeping Fenechka in the house without Arkady's permission, nor will he marry without Pavel's consent. He is incapable of dealing firmly with the peasants. He goes out of his way to avoid unpleasantness of any kind. Odintsova's life is a model of existence untouched by daring. Significantly, we learn in the epilogue that she has married a man who, like her, is cold as ice.

Bazarov, on the other hand, takes huge chances and endures the consequences. He flirts with Fenechka and as a result risks his life in a duel. He declares his "insane" love for Odintsova, is rejected, and is forced to reevaluate his view of life. Finally, he enters into a lethal flirtation with fate by not cauterizing the cut immediately. Bazarov's willingness to take such chances is a function of his all-embracing empiricism. As Muchnic expresses it, "Bazarov has the strength to act on his convictions and, in acting on them, proves them false."[7]

In the process of testing his views Bazarov reveals his vulnerability, a second key to his greatness. The confrontation with Odintsova demonstrates to Bazarov that he is not immune to passion. His fatal infection forces him to face up to the fact that he is not all-powerful, that he cannot negate death. It is his willingness to confront the truth, however distasteful it may be, that makes Bazarov so appealing. In other words—and this is a point often obscured in Turgenev criticism—Bazarov grows as a person immeasurably in the course of the novel. Matlaw writes:

> Bazarov denies the values of normal human behavior, but when his theory is put to a single test it collapses. . . . And in his illness Bazarov compresses into a brief period that acceptance of traditional values—family, love, life itself—that otherwise would accrue slowly and undramatically . . .[8]

The notion that Bazarov grows contradicts conventional wisdom regarding the post-Odintsova Bazarov. According to that view, his confrontation with Odintsova precipitates his disintegration and lapse into unrelieved pessimism. In fact, Bazarov is a pessimist throughout the novel. To be more precise, in the first part of *Fathers and Sons* Bazarov is personally self-assured but pessimistic about the world around him. His empirical mode of thought suggests to him that the world is in a chronic state of disrepair. In his discussions with Pavel, Bazarov is decidedly negative about the Russian peasantry, society, and its mores. He tells Pavel:

> I shall be prepared to agree with you when you present me with even a single aspect of our contemporary mode of life, whether familial or societal, that does not require complete and merciless negation. (274)

At the conclusion of the novel, Bazarov, empirically oriented as always, is no longer pessimistic about the world, but rather about his place in it. "My father may tell you what a loss I'll be to ... That's nonsense, but don't disillusion him" (396), he tells Odintsova. In the very fact of calling Odintsova to his deathbed Bazarov demonstrates that he is as susceptible to "romanticism" as anyone else. In other words, Bazarov grows in self-knowledge. The process is painful, but Bazarov endures it with dignity.

The fact that Bazarov changes over the course of the novel contradicts another popular truism about Turgenev's method of characterization. Most critics contend that there are no dynamic characters in Turgenev's works, that in his works character is revealed, but does not develop. Blair suggests that Turgenev's characters do not change, "rather the novelist makes them do things to reveal themselves completely."[9] Matlaw maintains that "Turgenev transmits character without really indicating its formation or progress."[10] Such statements are true if applied to anyone in *Fathers and Sons* except Bazarov and—with qualifications—Pavel. Odintsova's fruitless flirtation with Bazarov reveals her essential unwillingness or inability to commit herself to anyone or anything;

Arkady's romance with Katya reveals his true, and essentially static nature. Nikolay, Fenechka, Katya, and Bazarov's parents are presented as finished, relatively well-balanced personalities. In that sense, they are static characters. We do see change in Pavel, but we have only a fleeting glimpse of it in his pre-history; otherwise it is accurate to say that the duel reveals his essential emptiness. But what are we to say of Bazarov? To a certain extent it is foolhardy to speak of his enigmatic character at all, yet by the end of the novel we do know that Bazarov's initial cocksureness has been shattered, his attitudes about himself and his place in the world have been altered radically. He has discovered in himself feelings and attitudes whose existence he did not suspect. This sets him apart from someone like Arkady, who denies his real feelings throughout most of the novel. Bazarov, on the other hand, does not deny his feelings—he discovers them. If this is not change, what is?

Some critics are driven by this dynamism in Bazarov's characterization to speak of two Bazarovs. Pustovoit writes:

> Turgenev made so many changes [in Bazarov] after Odintsova that it was as if two different heroes arose before the reader. In any event the sharp break in Bazarov's character and in the whole line of his conduct became so perceptible that Turgenev rejected his original intentions to have the novel published in parts.[11]

It is true that Turgenev insisted that the novel be published in a single issue,[12] but nowhere did he ever suggest that the reason for this request was Bazarov's suddenly split personality.

Bazarov's decisive encounter with Odintsova, then, transforms him, leading to unexpected revelations about himself and the world. But that is hardly sufficient reason for speaking of two Bazarovs. Statements Bazarov makes in the final chapters are not consonant with those he makes in earlier chapters, but his contradictions are those of a living, thinking, developing human being: they are the stuff of life. Furthermore, the inconsistencies are subordinated to a larger overall consistency in Bazarov's characterization. Bazarov is ever the empiricist. He accepts nothing on faith: he recognizes the irrational power of love and the inevitability of death only when he is personally confronted by them.

Bazarov's greatness, then, tends toward the understatement of stoicism rather than the flamboyance of melodramatic displays.

As Muchnic observes:

> Bazarov is bigger than he shows himself to be. He is fine not because, but in spite of, his views and actions. His greatness is implicit; what he really is is a contradiction of what he represents himself to be. What is obvious in him is limited and unpleasant; what is hidden is big.[13]

A common feature of many analyses of Bazarov is a discussion of his historical prototypes. That question will be treated in a later chapter. In this chapter we will take up an aspect of Bazarov's characterization that is only rarely taken into consideration—his *literary* prototypes.

When we turn to the subject of Bazarov's literary prototypes, we find ourselves in almost virgin territory. Two Western scholar-critics, Edmund Wilson and Eva Kagan-Kans, have done work in this much neglected area. Wilson has suggested Yakov Pasynkov as one of Bazarov's literary prototypes:

> Later on, the description of Yakov Pasynkov in the story of that name is so similar to the description of Belinsky in the *Reminiscences* that it is evident that the latter had sat for Yakov, who dies of an injury to the lung, as both Belinsky and Stankevich died of tuberculosis. Now, "Yakov Pasynkov" is also a kind of preliminary study for the large-scale *Fathers and Sons,* and when we come to *Fathers and Sons,* we find that it is dedicated to the memory of Belinsky—who had died thirteen years before—and that its hero, like Belinsky himself, is the son of a poor army doctor and has a pitiful premature death.[14]

Demonstrating the links between Belinsky and Yakov Pasynkov is a commonplace of Soviet Turgenev criticism, but Wilson is the first and so far the only critic to extend the parallels to *Fathers and Sons*. Does a close reading of "Yakov Pasynkov," published in 1855, provide any support for Wilson's view? The answer is a qualified yes. Yakov is a tender Romantic—a representative of the 1840s—who loves poetry, friendship, Schubert, and a woman who barely knows that he exists. At the conclusion of the tale he suffers a fatal arrow wound (!) and dies personally unfulfilled, since all his life he has pined for a woman who remains oblivious of him. Throughout the tale Yakov is characterized as one of the last Romantics.

Without stretching the imagination too far, one can isolate seeds of *Fathers and Sons* here. Like Bazarov, Yakov is the strong, proud, silent type. Words never ring false on his lips. His father is a poor, retired military man. Yakov dies from an absurd wound, leaving his promise unfulfilled. All of this has conspicuous parallels with Bazarov as well as with Belinsky. And the penultimate line of the tale, "Peace to thy ashes, thou unpractical man, thou kindhearted idealist!" (VI, 234), cannot fail to evoke the final passage of *Fathers and Sons*. Yakov, though devoid of Bazarov's rebellion, is an obliquely preparatory portrait for the latter hero.

Kagan-Kans suggests "First Love," dating from 1860, as a tale with thematic links to *Fathers and Sons*. Specifically, she draws parallels between the narrator's father in "First Love" and Bazarov, pointing out that both "value their spiritual freedom above all else. Once they succumb to their passion, they perish."[15] Interestingly, Batyuto argues that the father resembles Pavel, not Bazarov.[16] There really is no contradiction here, however, since Pavel and Bazarov share enough character traits to make them variants of a single personality type.

Hamlet and Don Quixote are occasionally cited as Bazarov's literary prototypes. Fridlender and Batyuto call Bazarov "a combination of Don Quixote and Hamlet."[17] Yury Mann suggests that Bazarov is "a Hamletizing Don Quixote."[18] Freeborn writes that Bazarov is Turgenev's attempt at a Quixotic character and that Bazarov's death shows Turgenev's inability to reconcile Hamlet and Don Quixote.[19] Scholars are drawn to such conclusion by the fact that only two years before the appearance of *Fathers and Sons* Turgenev had published an essay, "Hamlet and Don Quixote."[20] Thus it seems not unlikely that Turgenev had these two characters somewhere in the back of his mind as he set to work on *Fathers and Sons*.

The fundamental tenet of "Hamlet and Don Quixote" (VIII, 169-192) is that the two characters represent two polarities of human nature: Hamlet embodies egoism, analysis, skepticism, lack of faith, and inability to act; Don Quixote stands for unquestioned and unquestioning faith that is translated into action. More specifically, Don Quixote believes in an ideal outside of himself which he does not analyze or doubt.[21] He does not know a lot, but he does not need to know a great deal: his faith sustains him.[22] As a result he is an enthusiast, a self-confident man of action who is prepared to lay down his life in defense of others. Furthermore, because of his faith in something outside himself, he is free from egoism and self-preoccupation. He is humorous and lovable. His social origins are lower class.

To what extent are these characteristics shared by Bazarov, especially the pre-Odintsova Bazarov, who presumably is then at his most Quixotic? The social origins are the same, and the Bazarov we see in the first few chapters of the novel is supremely self-confident. But even in those first few chapters it is apparent that Bazarov is an egoist who is excessively preoccupied with himself—witness his reluctance to shake Nikolay's hand or talk in the presence of the older Kirsanovs. Such items argue against Bazarov's portrait even as an attempt at a Quixotic hero. In addition, Bazarov lacks a Quixotic ideal for which he is ready to spring into action. The text confirms that Bazarov advocates negating "the old," i.e., the norms of contemporary social life. Bazarov's program calls for negation and destruction, but whether his methods will be violent or non-violent, organized or spontaneous—these things we do not know. Bazarov refuses to outline any positive, constructive plans. When Nikolay argues that one cannot merely destroy, that one must also build, Bazarov replies laconically: "That's not our business... First the place needs a clean sweep" (243). Bazarov's ideal—destruction and negation—is not an ideal in the sense in which Turgenev applies the word to Don Quixote.

Quixote is an enthusiast, a man of action; Bazarov seems to be a man contemplating preparing for action. His enthusiasm is very low-keyed: he speaks of militancy, but rarely displays it himself even in his speech, let alone actions. Note, for instance, that he regrets becoming expansive in his altercation with Pavel (245). Bazarov is perhaps a Quixotic type in his primitive single-mindedness, but he remains only potentially a man of action. Given the chance to destroy "the old," i.e., Pavel at the duel, he turns magnanimous. Furthermore, Bazarov is a contrast to Don Quixote in that most of his actions betray a profound indifference to the people and world around him, not a commitment to them.

Lastly, although Bazarov may at times strike us as funny (Who today can restrain a chuckle as Bazarov once again takes up with his beloved frogs?),[23] we hardly find him lovable. Pitiable, admirable, tragic, but scarcely lovable. Therefore, we must conclude that there is very little textual support for the notion that Bazarov is an attempt at a Russian Don Quixote.

Turgenev's interpretation of the character of Hamlet, on the other hand, helps to illuminate Bazarov. Hamlet, according to Turgenev, represents analysis, egoism, and lack of faith. He symbolizes negation. Specifically, his negation

> is not evil—it itself is directed against evil. Hamlet's negation doubts [the existence of good], but it does not doubt evil and enters into fierce battle with it. . . . Hamlet's scepticism, not believing in the contemporary version of truth, so to speak, belligerently does battle with falsehood and thereby becomes one of the main defenders of the truth in which it cannot entirely believe. (VIII, 183)

Turgenev's description of Hamlet's mode of disbelief is as accurate an analysis of Bazarov's views as one could hope for: we do not know what Bazarov believes in, but we do know what he opposes.[24]

Turgenev continues:

> But in negation, as in fire, there is a destructive force—and how is one to confine this force within boundaries, how is one to point out just where it should stop, when that which it should destroy and that which it should spare are often melded and linked inseparably? (VIII, 183)[25]

Turgenev goes on:

> Here is where appears the so often remarked tragic side of human life: for action one needs will, for action one needs thought: but thought and will have become disparate and become more so with every day. . . (VIII, 183)

This passage suggests that although there is very little of Don Quixote in Bazarov, Turgenev's essay is nonetheless a kind of philosophical prologue to the novel. The genetic link is clear if we compare Turgenev's remarks about the disjunction of thought and will with the epigraph which he considered and then rejected for the novel:

> Young person to a middle-aged person:
> "There was content in you, but no strength."
>
> Middle-aged person:
> "And in you there is strength without content."
> (From a contemporary conversation)
> (446)[26]

Additional traits that Bazarov shares with Turgenev's Hamlet include egoism, a tendency to analysis, and hatred of the masses. Bazarov's ego is wounded by Odintsova, and later, when Arkady asks him whether he cares what people think of him, Bazarov hedges on his answer: "I don't know what to tell you. A real man shouldn't care about it..." (324). We see his analytical turn of mind in the same conversation, as we had in an earlier one, when he broods about his insignificance before the universe and eternity (306, 323).[27] Hamlet-like in his contempt for the herd, Bazarov vents his hatred for Filip and Sidor, the peasants for whom he is "supposed to turn himself inside out" (325).[28]

There is only one passage in *Fathers and Sons* where we do see elements of both Don Quixote and Hamlet: that is the section describing Bazarov's death. Turgenev writes on the deaths of Hamlet and Don Quixote:

> Both Hamlet and Don Quixote die touchingly; but how different are their deaths! Hamlet's last words are beautiful. He is reconciled, grows calm, bids farewell to Horatio, raises his dying voice on behalf of the young Fortinbras, the unsoiled representative of the rights of inheritance... but Hamlet's gaze does not look ahead... "The rest...is silence," says the dying sceptic, and he really falls silent forever. Don Quixote's death arouses in us indescribable compassion. At that instant all of this great character's enormous significance becomes accessible to everyone. When his former squire, trying to make him feel better, says that they will soon be off again on knightly adventures: "No," answers the dying man, "all of that is gone forever, and I beg everyone's pardon; I am no longer Don Quixote, I am again Alonzo the Good, as they used to call me, Alonso el Bueno." (VIII, 191)

Several critics have noted that Bazarov's last words, "Enough. Now... darkness," recall Hamlet's "The rest is silence."[29] Turgenev's comments about Hamlet's gaze not looking ahead also reverberate in Bazarov's death scene, where for the first time in the novel Bazarov discusses his past and contrasts his former thoughts with his current beliefs. By contrast, Bazarov's renunciation of his great plans ("And I thought I'd accomplish a lot of things, I wouldn't die, no! There was a task, and after all I was a giant! And now the giant's entire task is to die decently..." [396]), and his refusal to respond affirmatively to his father's distraught assurances that he may yet recover—all of this recalls Quixote's death as Turgenev analyzes it.

Of interest in connection with Turgenev's essay is the fact that his interpretations of Hamlet and Don Quixote are hardly original: like many of Turgenev's ideas, they have their roots in German Romanticism. The image of Hamlet as a tortured intellectual reduced to a state of indecisive inertia because of his excessively developed powers of reflection was first propounded by such giants of German Romanticism as Goethe and August Schlegel.[30] The notion of Don Quixote as a positive, heroic figure also arose among the German Romantics: August Schlegel and Schopenhauer both stressed Quixote's epic aspects.[31] The affinity between Turgenev and the German Romantics regarding Hamlet and Don Quixote touches upon an interesting and rather neglected issue, that of Turgenev's debt to Romanticism.

Western scholars have recently begun to draw attention to the fact that Turgenev's literary roots are deeply imbedded in Romanticism. Eva Kagan-Kans and Marina Ledkovsky, in particular, have used Turgenev's short stories to demonstrate his links with Romanticism.[32] Such scholars as Alexander Fischler and William C. Brumfield have expanded the discussion to include Bazarov.[33]

Bazarov, for all his similarity to the decidedly anti-Romantic "new people" of the 1860s, comes to us more or less directly from the pages of Russian Romanticism. He is one of the last Romantic heroes in Russian literature. Specifically, Bazarov is the direct descendant of the rebel hero of European and Russian Romanticism, and in him the Byronic element is particularly strong.

Bazarov's general movement toward isolation, the principle of "one against all," as Yury Mann refers to it,[34] reveals the Romantic roots in *Fathers and Sons*. As Cornelius van Schooneveld observes:

> Even a cursory analysis of a few of the greatest Russian authors of the Romantic movement suffices to establish certain common denominators in the architecture of their works, especially regarding the relationship of the main hero to the other persons appearing in the narrative, and of the relationship of the hero and these personalities to the author.
>
> The relationship of the *first level* is developed in the story almost the way a bowling game evolves: one after the other, the hero eliminates the other persons from the scene in that he destroys their ability to influence actively the course of events. . . .

> The *second level*, that of the relationship between the author and his hero, is motivated by romantic irony. Just as the hero destroys his adversaries, finally the author, in an epilogue or by more subtle means, removes the hero of the story from the stage of the action.[35]

Bazarov's progress through the novel is not exactly like that of van Schooneveld's bowling ball, for he does not always eliminate people's ability to influence the course of events, although that is essentially what he does to Pavel. Instead, he eliminates people's ability to influence his own life. Thus he rejects the Kirsanovs and tries to stay away from Odintsova. His general movement, like that of the bowling ball, is toward isolation. And Turgenev does remove his solitary hero from the stage by the end of the novel. It is in part because of this structural similarity with the classics of Russian Romanticism that we have reason to consider Bazarov one of the last tragic Romantic heroes in Russian literature.

Mario Praz traces the origins of the rebel hero to Milton's *Paradise Lost:* "Toward the end of the eighteenth century Milton's Satan transfused with his own sinister charm the traditional type of the generous outlaw or sublime criminal."[36] Significantly, Turgenev confessed apropos of Bazarov's origins that he had "dreamed of some sort of strange *pendant* with Pugachev" as he conceived Bazarov (letter to Sluchevsky [4, 381]). Even more illuminating is Turgenev's statement about his favorite heroes: "Je préfère Promethée, je préfère Satan, le type de la révolte et de l'individualité" (1, 279).

As in the case of Byron's heroes, Lermontov's Vadim and Pechorin, Pushkin's Aleko, and others, Bazarov's origins are mysterious—prosaically so in his case—but all the same they are a puzzle. Bazarov, as noted earlier, is the only major character in *Fathers and Sons* whom Turgenev does not provide with a pre-history.[37] Critics have offered multiple explanations for this. Byaly makes a contradictory suggestion: Turgenev himself knew nothing about the origins of the new people, and giving Bazarov a suitable pre-history might have produced problems with the censors.[38] Reeve asserts that Bazarov has no biography because for him history is only in the future,[39] while Matlaw argues that Bazarov "lives exclusively in the present."[40] All of these explanations may be correct in part, but surely the major reason Turgenev gives Bazarov no pre-history is that this simple device immediately sets him off from the other characters, at once emphasizing his isolation and status as a stranger. More importantly, it increases the air of mystery surrounding Bazarov. That mystery, of course, is a crucial feature of the Romantic rebel.

The rebel's aura of mystery is often intensified by his silence. Of Byron's Lara ("Lara"), for instance, we learn that

> His silence formed a theme for others' prate—
> They guessed—they gazed—they fain would know his fate.[41]

Bazarov is very laconic: especially in the early chapters of *Fathers and Sons* he is wrapped in a silence only occasionally punctuated by his pithy, iconoclastic observations.[42]

Bazarov is also reminiscent of the Romantic hero in his status as the proud outsider who sweepingly scorns all. Bazarov enters the novel as the aloof unknown superior. He is the stranger at Marino who barely deigns to shake Nikolay's hand. He dies more an outsider than ever: "Does Russia need me? No, clearly she does not" (396), he tells Odintsova.[43] Thus, by the conclusion of the novel the boundaries within which Bazarov feels himself alienated have extended appreciably—from Marino to all of Russia. Bazarov's scorn for humanity and things human is everywhere apparent, nowhere more than in his previously mentioned self-appraisal: "When I meet a man who doesn't give in to me... then I'll change my opinion of myself" (325).

Allied with the rebel hero's lofty contempt for the world one usually finds a love of solitude, often expressed in voluntary exile or extended wanderings.[44] One observes that Bazarov spends much of his time at Marino alone with his microscope and frogs, while he leaves his parents' home after having spent only three days there: his parents would not leave him in peace. Restless, frequently on the move, he feels at ease nowhere, as may be deduced from his travels. At the Kirsanovs' he spends his first morning wandering around the estate in search of frogs. His appearance at breakfast recalls that of the perpetual itinerant:

> His linen jacket and trousers were covered with mud; a clinging marsh plant had twined itself around the crown of his old round hat; in his right hand he held a small sack . . . .(217)

Upon his return home at the close of the novel, he spends the first several days closeted away in his room. He has submitted himself to voluntary exile, withdrawal from the world.

In all the traits shared by Bazarov and the Romantic rebel there is an air of chronic adolescence. Their characters combine the petulance, arrogance, brashness, self-complacency, rejection of sentiment, and narcissistic self-absorption which literature and life confirm as typically adolescent. As Matlaw observes: "Bazarov's two big traits are his immaturity and his position as an outsider in 'a world he never made.' They make him attractive and repellent."[45]

Like the rebel hero, especially the "fatal" hero, Bazarov follows a general course of progressive rejection of others, culminating in his own rejection, i.e., annihilation by the author. Praz notes: "Romantic heroes destroy others around them, themselves, and the women they love."[46] We have had cause earlier to mention van Schooneveld's similar "bowling ball" analysis of the Romantic hero's actions.[47] According to Ostrovskaia, Turgenev remarked that Bazarov had to die because he did not know what else to do with him.[48] Turgenev may have been sincere in this pronouncement (if in fact he ever made it), but on a formal level he was merely following the conventional pattern for the Romantic rebel's life and inevitable death.

Another important point linking Bazarov with the Romantic hero is the nature of the process whereby Bazarov is broken. It involves his exposure and rapidly developed susceptibility to irrational forces, largely in the form of love—a confrontation that has sobering and ultimately shattering consequences for him.[49] This is one of the archetypal patterns of German Romanticism. E. T. A. Hoffmann's stories (and those of his Russian disciple, Odoevsky), for instance, abound in the motif. In its more extreme formulations the confrontation with Beauty is equated with Death.[50] The motifs of love, Beauty, and death converge in Bazarov's last meeting with Odintsova. He gazes at her and says:

> Well, what can I tell you... I loved you! Even then that had no significance, and even less now. Love is a form, and my own form is already disintegrating. I'm better off saying that—how lovely you are! And now there you stand, so beautiful... (395)

Finally, Turgenev himself admitted that there was something of the Romantic in Bazarov. Writing of *Virgin Soil* he remarked:

> There are Romantics of Realism.... They long for a reality and strive toward it, as former Romantics did toward the ideal. In reality they seek not poetry—that is ludicrous for them—but something grand and meaningful; and that's nonsense: real life is prosaic and should be so .... They are preachers and prophets in their own way, but complete prophets, contained and defined in themselves. Preaching is an illness, a hunger, a desire; a healthy person cannot be a prophet or even a preacher. Therefore I put something of *that* Romanticism in Bazarov too, but only Pisarev noticed it (XII, 314-315).[51]

The phrase "Romantics of Realism" is very helpful for understanding the basis of Bazarov's characterization. What Turgenev has done in *Fathers and Sons* is to take the traditional Romantic hero and prosaicize him without ultimately depriving him of his grandeur and interest. Bazarov does not cut the striking figure that we associate with Byron's or Lermontov's heroes. He enters the novel neither on horseback nor at the helm of a ship, but in a dust-covered carriage. His clothing is shabby and not the least bit exotic. Bazarov's face is "long and thin, with a wide brow, flat at the top, with a pointed nose toward the bottom, large greenish eyes, and sidewhiskers of a sandy color..." (200). Such is hardly the face of a hero, though it expresses the "self-assurance and intelligence" (200) that we expect of the Romantic hero. Bazarov's locus of activity is neither the dramatically beautiful Caucasus so favored by Pushkin and Lermontov nor the mysterious, dangerous Middle East populated by Byron's protagonists: it is the most commonplace of settings—ramshackle Russian estates and a tacky provincial town. The woman with whom Bazarov is involved is neither a noble savage, an enslaved beauty, nor a woman of society: she is the self-sufficient, complacent Odintsova. The duel in *Fathers and Sons,* a stock feature of Romantic fiction, is surrounded by comic details. It is not a scene designed to make the reader palpitate with excitement and terror, but Bazarov nonetheless risks his life in the duel. In short, Bazarov manifests the typical traits of the Romantic hero; his actions, as we have seen, parallel those of the typical Romantic hero; but Turgenev conceals Bazarov's literary origins by painting him in drab colors and placing him in an environment normally thought of as alien to the Romantic hero. Curiously, Bazarov's links with the Byronic hero are encoded within his own speech. When Arkady asks Bazarov, "But the truth—where is it, on which side?", Bazarov answers: "Where?

I'll answer you like an echo: where?" (VIII, 324). His reply is a paraphrase of the line "And Echo answers—'Where'" from Byron's "Bride of Abydos" (Canto II, Stanza XXVII).

These remarks hardly exhaust the topic of Bazarov's characterization, but remaining comments are more germane to later chapters. Therefore, let us move on to a consideration of the other characters in *Fathers and Sons.*

Nikolay's natural environment, as it were, is the diminutive. Most of these forms are untranslatable, so I will merely point out several examples of words which, in the Russian text, are diminutives. In his childhood Nikolay was called "scaredy-cat" *(trusishka,* 196); later he broke his leg and remained lame *(khromenky,* 196) for life. The first description we find of his estate abounds in diminutives (here marked by asterisks):

> One also came upon streams* with carved out banks, tiny* ponds with thin dikes, villages* with low huts* under roofs that were often half swept away, tumbledown threshing sheds* with wattled walls. . . . (205)

The use of diminutives in such quantities eventually impresses us not as affection, but condescension. Neither Nikolay nor his estate seems to be part of the adult world, or so the diminutives suggest.

In fact Nikolay does not cope very well with the world. His ill luck is a constant motif: on the day he is to enter the military he breaks his leg (197); his idyllic marriage is cut short by his wife's sudden death (197); his desire to go abroad to exorcise his grief is circumvented by the revolutions of 1848. He eagerly awaits his beloved son's return home, only to discover that Arkady is a nihilist who dismisses his father's generation. Things in general do not go well on the estate: the trees that Nikolay plants do not really take, the pond he builds fails to fill with enough water, and the water from the well he has ordered dug has a brackish taste (211). His attempts to turn his estate into a model progressive farm are hardly successful: the peasants do not pay the levies on time (if at all) and Nikolay is constantly short of cash. Interestingly, Nikolay's problems with converting his estate into a farm parallel Turgenev's own.[52] Another point linking Nikolay with his creator is their mutual readiness to surrender to the new generation. Nikolay tells Pavel: "Yes, brother; it's clearly time for us to order coffins and fold our arms across out chests" (240). Compare this sentiment with a similar one in Turgenev's letter to Fet, written during the time he was composing *Fathers and Sons* and reacting to Dobroliubov's rejection of the men of the 1840s:

> So now you and I have fallen in with the Podolinskys, Trilunys, and other respected retired majors. What are we to do, old man! It's time to give way to the young ones. (4, 125)

In general Nikolay is akin to Turgenev in his love of nature, poetry, and music, his inability to cope effectively with estate management, his concern with how the young view him, and his willingness to consider all sides of an issue. He is unlike Turgenev in that even though he copes poorly with the world, he is granted two happy marriages, a loving son, and his own "nest."

There is an interesting, though minor technical problem with Nikolay's age. When first introduced to Nikolay, we learn that he is a little over forty *(let soroka s nebolshim,* 195). This is the case both in the Paris manuscript and in the canonical text. A few chapters later in the Paris mansucript Nikolay is suddenly forty-eight (454). This was changed to forty-four in the canonical text, but it indicates a general problem that Turgenev had in keeping track of his secondary characters' ages, one we shall encounter again when we come to Katya.

Byaly argues that Pavel is un-Russian, that he has no ties to Russia, that his affair with Princess R. "places the hero ... outside the national elements of Russian life."[53] Byaly's statement is essentially inane (Is Turgenev also un-Russian?), but there is an element of truth in it. Pavel's speech, for instance, is distinctly uncolloquial Russian. It is that of an aristocrat who is never completely at home in Russian. He affects certain pseudo-elegant aristocratic mispronunciations (*efto* for *eto,* 247, and *prinsíp* for *príntsip,* 216) and generally relies on old-fashioned turns of speech. At times his Russian is downright unidiomatic. When he says to Bazarov, "And now, my dear sir, all that remains for me is to thank you and return you to your studies (*vozvratit vas vashim zaniatiam,* 349)" he relies on a turn of speech that is so formal as to be un-Russian.[54] It sounds very much like a subconscious translation from French or English, the latter hypothesis supported by the Anglophile aura surrounding Pavel. Note that at the time of the action of the novel Pavel reads more and more English works (225), and at the conclusion of Chapter IV we find him with the latest issue of *Galignani's Messenger*,[55] an English-language newspaper published in Paris. In general Pavel's speech is instantly recognizable: it is as elegant, fastidious, and hyper-correct as his dress, the furnishings in his room, and the man himself.

It is ironic that although Pavel protests the use of force, it is he who introduces a note of violence into the novel by challenging Bazarov to the duel. Much has been written about the duel, but there is no broad agreement as to the meaning either of its occurrence or its outcome. Gifford states, for instance, that "Bazarov's duel with Pavel Petrovich over Fenechka has no significance other than one that is broadly ideological."[56] This is perhaps an extreme view, but it is shared by Freeborn, Howe, Vinogradov, and Fisher, among others.[57] Although we are dealing with an ideological novel, we do Turgenev a disservice in assuming that every personage and every act of the novel is to be understood exclusively in terms of ideology. *Fathers and Sons* is ultimately of more interest for what it has to say about the human condition (or at least Turgenev's view of it) than for its insights into the ideological struggles of the 1860s. The duel displays the depth of Pavel's attraction to Fenechka, who reminds him of Princess R., and suggests that in Turgenev's world the erotic memory is extraordinarily long-lived. Thus for Pavel the impulse for the duel is as much erotic as ideological and in fact suggests that ideology takes a back seat to feeling as a motivation for human behavior. Bazarov's participation in the duel is a function of his pride, which Pavel has managed to pique at last. As Bazarov observes to himself after accepting the challenge:

> "And it would have been impossible to refuse; after all he probably would have struck me, and then... (Bazarov turned pale at the very thought; all his pride reared up on end.) Then I would have had to strangle him, like a kitten." (349)

Finally, the duel reveals that neither Pavel nor Bazarov is really a bad sort. Bazarov, given a chance to carry out the destruction that he preaches, declines the opportunity. Both he and Pavel display generosity after the duel, Bazarov caring for his wounded "patient," and Pavel urging his brother to marry Fenechka. Thus, the duel has a meaning other than an ideological one—it illuminates character. Furthermore, it plays an important structural role in *Fathers and Sons*. As Blair point out, "At the end of the duel, Bazarov and Pavel are alone and separated from the normal flow of life."[58] In structural terms, they have both been removed from the comedic plot line, while Bazarov is firmly on the path to the culmination of the tragic line.[59] In this sense both Bazarov and Pavel lose the duel. None of this is to deny that the duel has ideological significance, but that side of the question will be treated in the chapter on *Fathers and Sons* and the 1860s.[60]

Katya is probably the least discussed, least appreciated character in *Fathers and Sons*. Critics tend to ignore, dismiss, or denigrate her. Yet she is a fascinating type. As suggested earlier, Katya is one of the novel's observers. She says little, but her silences speak volumes. As Batyuto points out about her conduct during Bazarov and Odintsova's conversation in Chapter XVI:

> During this entire conversation Katya says literally not a single word, she only looks at Bazarov and Arkady, now "frowningly," now with "bewilderment"; but it is exactly these glances that testify that she is following the conversation intently, silently taking part in it and also does not agree with the "nihilists." Turgenev in this way gives us to understand that the hardly noticeable Katya, who is almost a little girl, has independence of mind, independence of character.[61]

When Katya does occasionally break silence, she reveals herself to be "sensible and very shrewd in her assessment of others," as Boyd puts it.[62] In this connection it is worth recalling that it is Katya who tells Arkady that both he and her sister had been under Bazarov's influence, that both are now free of it, and that Arkady cannot wish to be anything other than what he is (364-365). Katya occupies a unique position in the novel in that she cannot easily be counted a full member of any of the major groups into which the characters seem naturally to fall. She is not as strong as Bazarov, Pavel, or her sister, yet she is appreciably stronger than any of the meek characters. Significantly, in the Paris manuscript the narrator tells us that Bazarov did not even suspect that "There was in her [Katya] much firmness of a sort" (460/286). Katya adores music, poetry, and nature, yet one senses that her commitment to them is somehow less elemental than Arkady's or Nikolay's. She does not lack an inner life—she has a habit of retreating into herself (287)—yet the quality of the inner life remains undefined. There is a sense of incompleteness in Katya's portrait, perhaps because, as Fisher argues, Turgenev largely ignores the psychology of characters who are alien to him—Katya, for instance.[63] Katya is in many ways a compromise character: she represents a mid-point between her sister's intelligence, independence, and spiritual emptiness and Arkady's plain common sense, malleability, and spiritual health. In short, she seems well-balanced, and is perhaps therefore alien to her creator.

An illustration of what may be Turgenev's indifference to his heroine is his failure to keep track of her age. Boyd's observation that her age is not clear is a bit inaccurate.[64] Her age is definitely either eighteen or twenty-one. We know that Odintsova is twenty-nine (266). We also know that when Odintsova was twenty, Katya was twelve (270). Thus, Katya would seem to be twenty-one at the time of the novel's action. On the other hand, Turgenev tells us that she is eighteen (275).[65]

Odintsova, according to Kagan-Kans, is one of Turgenev's predatory heroines, "each [of whom] causes or tries to cause the destruction of the man entangled in her meshes."[66] But since Odintsova seeks very little besides peace and freedom, it might be more appropriate to rank her as an infernal woman. If Dostoevsky's heroines leap to mind at the mention of infernal women, that is as it should be, because Odintsova prefigures those Dostoevsky heroines who, like herself, have contradictory motivations and who ultimately seem in doubt about what it is they really want.[67] Although Turgenev relates details about Odintsova's inner life and character in several passages (271, 282, 283, 287, 300, and 373), much of this information is qualified by phrases such as "it seemed" *(kazalos)* and "as if" *(slovno)*. Thus, although the attention devoted to Odintsova's psyche is substantial, she nonetheless remains a mystery. Though her motivations are analyzed, they are not really explained. Turgenev uses a variation of a Gogolian technique for characterizing her: he piles up information which is ultimately less than illuminating. Consider, for instance, the lengthy description of Odintsova's character:

> Anna Sergeievna was a rather strange creature. Having no prejudices, not having any strong beliefs, she gave way to no one and had no direction of her own. She saw many things clearly, many things in-

terested her, but nothing satisfied her completely; and it is doubtful that she desired complete satisfaction. Her mind was questioning and indifferent at one and the same time: her doubts never calmed themselves to the point of forgetfulness and never reached the proportions of alarm. Had she not been wealthy and independent, she might perhaps have thrown herself into the fray, known passion... But she lived easily, although she was bored at times, and she continued to pass day after day without hurrying and only occasionally becoming upset. Iridescent colors sometimes flared up before her eyes, but she relaxed when they died down, and did not regret them. Her imagination would carry her even beyond the limits of what is considered allowable according to the laws of usual morals; but even then her blood flowed calmly as before in her enchantingly well-shaped and calm body....

Like all women who have not managed to love, she wanted something, she herself not knowing exactly what. In fact she wanted nothing, though it seemed to her that she wanted everything. She had scarcely tolerated the deceased Odintsov . . . and developed a secret revulsion toward all men... . . . Once somewhere abroad she had met a young handsome Swede with a face of knightly expression, with honest light blue eyes under an open brow; he made a strong impression on her, but that did not prevent her from returning to Russia. (282-283)

This passage reveals several things. The multiplicity of contradictions and the extensive use of indefinite pronouns *(chto-to, gde-to, kakoy-to)* have the effect of reducing Odintsova's seemingly complex personality to a zero. We should note that an examination of the Paris manuscript reveals that most of the passage just cited (from "Anna Sergeievna was a rather strange creature..." to "though it seemed to her that she wanted everything") was an afterthought on Turgenev's part (459). Annenkov, having read the first draft of *Fathers and Sons,* cautioned Turgenev about Odintsova's portrait: "This character is drawn by you so subtly that it is doubtful that future judges will completely understand her" (574-575). The introduction of new information about Odintsova seems to have been an attempt to bring her portrait into sharper focus. The added traits have the effect of making Odintsova both more mysterious and empty. Blair points out: "Whereas she [Odintsova] appears to be a lively, intelligent, mysterious, passionate woman, there is nothing at the core. Her emotions are dead."[68] Moreover, just as Pavel's experience with the Princess R. foreshadows Odintsova's effect on Bazarov, so the incident with the handsome Swede foretells Bazarov's effect on Odintsova. As

Kagan-Kans tells us, "Though she [Odintsova] brings destruction to Bazarov, she herself is untouched by any emotion; she is still lying under a blanket of snow and will always remain so."[69] Turgenev, in a letter to Sluchevsky, made a similar remark about his heroine: "She would first like to stroke the fur of a wolf (Bazarov), as long as he didn't bite—and then a boy's curls [Arkady's] — and to continue lying, freshly washed, on velvet" (4, 381).

Odintsova's interest in Arkady is rarely mentioned in existing critical material. Odintsova's transferral of attention to Arkady is a result of her experience with Bazarov. She has not been completely unaffected by him. He has taught her an important lesson—not to play with wolves. And just as the wounded Bazarov takes refuge in a flirtation with Fenechka—a romance which he knows cannot really touch his bruised ego, so the chastened Odintsova focuses on a much less dangerous male of the species, Arkady. Her interest in him is tactical, in a sense. In the first draft of the novel Odintsova's reorientation was not entirely clear. Annenkov, after reading the first draft, told Turgenev that he was too subtle on this point:

> Only in one place does it [Odintsova's portrait] become cloudy, i.e., in Chapter XXV, where Anna Sergeievna in her conversation with Bazarov expresses her new inclination toward Arkady. Here the lines are so thin that for their understanding one requires a mental magnifying glass, which not every person may have. It seems that you ought to hint at her new psychological state with some strong turn *(oborot)*.... (575)

The result was the passage in which Odintsova tells Bazarov:

> You say that he [Arkady] is not indifferent to me, and I myself always thought that he liked me. I know that I can only be an aunt to him, but I don't want to hide from you the fact that I have begun to think more often of him. In that young and fresh feeling there is a sort of delight.... (377)

When Odintsova shows Bazarov Arkady's letters of proposal to Katya, Odintsova pales, blushes, and laughs nervously (378-379). Thus, although Turgenev's description of Odintsova's essential indifference to Bazarov and Arkady is accurate, there is reason to believe that wounded vanity and a pronounced preference for marriages of convenience might have led her to marry Arkady: within the novel we see that she marries only men who represent no threat to her. In short, there is good reason to believe that Arkady barely escapes Odintsova's clutches. But are Katya's clutches any less destructive than her sister's? Is it true, as Kagan-Kans argues, that "the powers of a young virgin and a cruel woman are identical"?[70] There are two passages in *Fathers and Sons* which indicate that Katya has constructive designs on Arkady (admittedly, constructive designs may be as dangerous as destructive ones). At one point she tells Arkady, "Just wait, we'll make you over (*peredelaem*)" (364). She intends to transform the nihilist Arkady into the "domesticated animal" (365) that he really is. In the context of the novel, however, Arkady's transformation is a sign of health, and Katya's role in it can only be lauded. Later in the same chapter, after Odintsova has commented on her sister's exquisite little feet (*prelestnye nozhki*), we find the following:

> "Exquisite feet," she thought, slowly and lightly walking up the stone steps of the terrace that had been heated up by the sun, "exquisite feet, you say... Well, he [Arkady] will be at them."
> But she immediately felt ashamed and nimbly ran up [the steps]. (369)

Taken out of context, this passage gives cause for alarm, but considered as part of the whole novel, it only underscores the shrewdness of Katya's power of observation and suggests that she realizes that she is stronger than Arkady. Katya does tame Arkady, but in so doing she hardly destroys him. On the contrary, she saves him. The cited passage also indicates that there is considerably more to Katya than there appears on the surface. Her words run so counter to her limited and innocent image that their appearance here forces us to extend dramatically our reading of her.

As many commentators have pointed out,[71] the portrait of Bazarov's parents is essentially humorous. Their situation, however, is the most tragic of anyone's in the novel. The generation conflict in the Kirsanov family, for instance, is easily settled, since it has never really existed. But in the Bazarov family we see the generation conflict as it affects family relations. Bazarov is brusque and at times even rude with his parents, in spite of their constant attempts to please him. All of their efforts involve role-playing and self-denial: Arina hardly dares touch or talk to her son, while Vasily goes out of his way to play the "man without prejudices"

(328). The same things go on at the Kirsanovs', but by the end of the novel all the Kirsanovs have dropped their masks and are free to be themselves. The Bazaravs are "liberated" only by their son's death—a development that is signalled when Vasily at lasts drops his facade of atheism and begs his dying son to accept the last rites (392).

Vasily and Arina are essentially minor, vaguely humorous characters, yet Vasily's frenzied outburst, "Pray, Arina, pray!... Our son is dying!" (390), remains one of the most powerful and touching scenes in the novel.

We ought not to conclude our remarks without devoting at least minimal attention to imagery in the novel as it relates to both characterization and thematics. The most important images in *Fathers and Sons* are those relating to heat (fire, flames) and time. The fire and heat imagery links the themes of love and death, which Petrovsky identifies as two of the prime movers in Turgenev's world; the time imagery is related to fate, a third irrational element that connects the first two.[72] The fire and flame imagery was touched on earlier, in the second chapter, but it is worth noting that such imagery is introduced very early in the novel, where it is allied with passion:

> In Baden he [Pavel] took up with her [Princess R.] as before; it seemed he had never before loved her so passionately... but in a month everything was over: the fire (*ogon'*) flared up for the last time and died out forever. (334)[73]

The main action of the novel is played out under the hot summer sun, summer being the conventional literary season of passion. Those characters who are not susceptible to Turgenevian passion seek out the shade. As Arkady and his father ride toward Marino, Arkady remarks, "We have no shade, that's too bad" (202). Nikolay also complains about the lack of shade (342). Fenechka complains of the terrible heat which prevents her from going out of the house at any time other than the early morning. Arkady and Katya spend as much time as possible in the shade, either in the garden (363) or the gallery (374). In short, the Kirsanovs—father, sons, and their wives—know love but not passion (and, in Turgenev's world, are capable of happiness precisely because of that).

Most of the fire and heat imagery is radiated by the novel's most passionate character, Bazarov. On the evening before he confesses his love to Odintsova, he squeezes her hand with such force that she nearly cries out, and then he leaves. "She raised her crushed together *(skleivshiesia)* fingers to her lips, blew on them" (294). Odintsova's gesture is that of someone cooling his burned fingers. The essentially icy Odintsova is soon calmed, however:

> The lamp still burned for a long time in Anna Sergeievna's room, and for a long time she remained motionless, only occasionally running her fingers along her arms, which the night cold was lightly nipping. (295)

On the next day Bazarov, after proclaiming his love for Odintsova, leans his head against the window pane (299), as if trying to cool his fevered brow.

In a later conversation with Arkady, Bazarov himself identifies passion with heat. As he and Arkady ride towards Bazarov's home, Bazarov says:

> You won't believe me now, but I'm telling you: you and I fell into female company, and we had a nice time; but to leave such company is the same thing as dousing oneself with cold water on a hot day. (307)

The imagery which has thus far signified passion becomes identified with death when Bazarov falls ill. As soon as Timofeich has been dispatched to bring Odintsova, a cruel fever *(zhestoky zhar)* begins to torment Bazarov (391). During his death bed interview with Odintsova, Bazarov becomes confused and places his hand on his brow (396). Thus Turgenev again underlines Bazarov's fever and through the use of associative logic links it to the metaphorical fever that afflicted Bazarov at Nikolskoe. In his last words Bazarov asks Odintsova to "blow on the dying lamp, and let it die" (386). The logic of the imagery in the novel almost demands that Bazarov do this, that he ask the icy Odintsova to blow out the flame, thus extinguishing his passion with death. That the consequences of passion are death is emphasized in the final lines of the chapter:

> But the noontime heat *(znoy)* passes, evening and night come, and then a return to the quiet refuge, where the exhausted and tired sleep sweetly. (397)

Significantly, Bazarov's original declaration of love is made sometime around noon (299).

In *Fathers and Sons* time, its subjective apprehension and its objective flow, are central themes. All the characters are defined by their relation to time. Nikolay and Pavel are contrasted by the way ten years of their lives pass: for Nikolay, living with his beloved wife, they pass idyllically, like a dream (198); for Pavel, suffering the pangs of a lost love, the same ten years rush by with alarming speed, "colorlessly, fruitlessly" (224). Nikolay lives in the past, he constantly reminisces about his dead wife, while he tries half-heartedly to keep up with the present. Pavel, on the other hand, lives outside of time: "Having lost his past, he had lost everything" (224). His mode of existence is an attempt to arrest the passage of time. Odintsova tries to organize time: her entire household runs on a strict schedule (284-285). Arkady and Bazarov enjoy themselves so much at Nikolskoe that they lose all track of time.

Early in the novel Bazarov says, "And as for time, why should I depend on it? Better it should depend on me" (226). What Bazarov learns in the course of the novel is that everything and everyone on earth is dependent upon time; as in Tolstoy's world, time takes its toll and delivers its bounties, it changes people. Ultimately time is synonymous with fate.

Turgenev frequently emphasizes the power of time to alter people. Bazarov notices that his father has gone gray in the three years that have elapsed since he last saw him (307). When Bazarov leaves home after only three days, "Vasily Ivanovich . . .embraced his wife, his friend, more strongly than ever he had embraced her in his youth: she had comforted him in his sorrow" (334). Fenechka enters a new time in her life: "There is an epoch in the life of a young woman when they suddenly begin to bloom and flower like summer roses; such an epoch had arrived for Fenechka" (341).

Time transforms Bazarov and also kills him—both figuratively and literally. His post-Odintsova depression is reflected in his pessimistic meditations about time and eternity:

> And I think: here I lie under a hay stack... The narrow little space that I occupy is so tiny in comparison with the rest of space, where I am not and that has nothing to do with me; and the part of time which I will manage to live out is so insignificant before eternity, where I was not and won't be... And in this atom, in this mathematical point my

blood circulates, my brain works, it also wants something... What a mess! What nonsense! (323)

Bazarov dies because he waits four hours to apply an antiseptic to the cut incurred while performing an autopsy on a person who had died of typhus. Whether this is an act of fate pure and simple, or whether it is the more complex, but equally fateful matter of Russian roulette remains an unanswerable question, but it is time—the brief span of four hours—that ensures Bazarov's demise. In his deathbed speech Bazarov voices his discovery that time is wholly independent of him: he is its pawn. "Yes, just try to negate death," he tells his father, "it negates you, and that's that." Paradoxically, however, Bazarov's coming to terms with time's invincible might is a function not of the working of the cosmic clock that ticks away objectively throughout most of the novel, but rather of Turgenev's sudden acceleration of time. As Matlaw suggests:

> Normally the problem of generations is solved by time: the sons gradually move toward their permanent positions, give over being "angry young men," and become husbands and fathers, angry or not.... And in his brief illness Bazarov compressed into a brief period that acceptance of traditional values—family, love, life itself—that otherwise would accrue slowly and undramatically.[74]

At the conclusion of the novel Pavel has lost his past (224), Bazarov his future, and the Kirsanovs—father and son—who neither try to counteract time nor ignore it, continue living in the everlasting present.

Here we conclude our remarks about characterization in *Fathers and Sons* as an autonomous work of imaginative literature. In the preceding chapter and the present one we have attempted to confine the discussion of characterization to matters that are inherent in the text itself and do not depend on a larger context for their elucidation. (In demonstrating that Bazarov is a Romantic hero *manqué* we admit to having gone outside the text, but this chapter seemed the most appropriate place for such an analysis.) As we shall see in subsequent chapters, what has already been noted can be enlarged upon considerably by appealing to such contexts as the socio-historical background for the novel and the novel's links to works that preceded and succeeded it.

IV

FATHERS AND SONS AND THE 1860s

There is no doubt that Turgenev intended *Fathers and Sons* as a portrait of the Russian intelligentsia of the late 1850s and early 1860s (which for the sake of convenience will be referred to henceforth as the 1860s). In all his novels Turgenev voluntarily complied with Belinsky's demand for a literature of social comment. In an introduction to the 1880 edition of his collected novels, Turgenev described his goals as a writer in the following way:

> During all this time I have been aiming, to the extent that my strength and intelligence have sufficed, conscientiously and impartially to depict and embody in appropriate types what Shakespeare calls "the body and pressure of time" and the quickly changing physiognomy of Russians of the cultured stratum, which has served preeminently as the object of my observations. (X, 292)

The era of the 1860s was one of conflict. Turgenev had only recently broken with *The Contemporary (Sovremennik)*, whose editorial board included such radical firebrands as Chernyshevsky and Dobroliubov and which was adopting an increasingly radical orientation.[1] The immediate reason for Turgenev's rift with the journal was his irritation with Dobroliubov's article "When Will the Real Day Come?", which implied that Turgenev's *On the Eve* was an exhortation to revolution. But there were more profound reasons for the break, which was emblematic of the polarization then under way among the Westernizing intelligentsia. The sources of the polarization were many, but in essence it was a clash between two generations—the generation of the 1840s and the so-called "new people" of the 1860s. Underlying the generation gap were social and ideological arguments. The men of the 1840s, with some notable exceptions, were of the gentry class; the men of the 1860s tended to be *raznochintsy*.[2] The generation of the 1840s was inclined to see the world through the prism of German Idealism; the politics of the Westernizers owed much to English Liberalism. The men of the 1860s rejected Idealism in favor of Materialism, art in favor of science, and gradual reform in favor of revolution. Thus the first task in this chapter will be to examine the roots of *Fathers and Sons* in the era of the 1860s. Here it would be well to repeat what was noted elsewhere: in *Fathers and Sons* Turgenev transmutes the generational, ideological, and social conflicts of the 1860s into clashes of temperament and personality. The historical facts of the era provide the superficial subject matter of the novel. Turgenev's genius manifests itself in *Fathers and Sons* in his ability to combine the topical and the universal, and he does so by making the topical a function of the universal. Thus he avoids the trap into which many writers fall when they attempt to convince us that their topical concerns are universal.[3]

The second task in this chapter will be to determine Turgenev's stance vis-à-vis the social conflicts he portrays in the novel. Turgenev claimed that he was an objective writer, that his novels were portraits of, not comments on their age. He defined an objective writer in this way:

> If the study of a human physiognomy, another person's life, interests you *more* than outlining your own feelings and thoughts; if, for example, it is more *enjoyable* for you to convey truthfully and precisely the external appearance not only of a person, but of a simple thing, than to express elegantly and ardently what you experience upon seeing that thing or person, that means you are an objective writer and can undertake a *povest* or a novel. (11, 279-280)

Turgenev's notion of objectivity will not stand up to analysis—objectivity is the reader's illusion and an author's device—but the point is that Turgenev was against tendentious literature. He railed at Fet when the latter accused him of a "tendency" in *Fathers and Sons:* "Tendency! But what tendency is there in *Fathers and Sons,* allow me to ask?" (4, 371). Turgenev's protestations, principles, and intentions to the contrary, his novel is a statement about the era that produced it. (Turgenev occasionally admitted as much, although, as we shall see, many of the things he had to say were, as ever, contradictory.) Turgenev's judgement on his age is ambivalent, but not ambiguous.

Bazarov is in part a literary edition of what Turgenev perceives as the typical radical of the 1860s. Pavel and Nikolay, in various ways and to varying degrees, typify the generation of the 1840s. Bazarov and his parents are *raznochintsy;* Pavel and

Nikolay are of the gentry. These social distinctions are evident to the social historian in the speech and interests of these characters. Pavel and Nikolay both know several foreign languages: they lard their speech with English, French, and German phrases. Nikolay and Arkady conduct a lengthy conversation in French (203-204). Their language is representative of the Russian gentry of the day. Bazarov and his father, on the other hand, pepper their conversation with Latinisms and Classical allusions. In this way, as Malia points out, their speech is typical of the *raznochintsy*, who were trained in seminaries and *gimnazii,* and whose first (and often only) foreign language was Latin.[4] We recall, for instance, that Vasily proves incapable of carrying on a conversation in German with the doctor whom Odintsova brings with her (394). The social distinctions between the two families also surface in their musical tastes. Nikolay loves Schubert, Arkady likes Mozart, but Vasily hums Meyerbeer (321), whose operas are generally considered the nadir of French music, and who made his career by catering to the tastes of the French bourgeoisie.[5] Class differences in the novel are further underscored in the characterization of Bazarov's mother, whose ardent religiosity, superstitiousness, and lack of the conventional social graces set her off from the refined Katya and Odintsova. It was Turgenev who, in a letter, described Odintsova as "a representative of our idle, dreaming, curious, and cold epicurean gentry ladies" (4, 381).

Since much of Bazarov's behavior and many of his expressed views are typical of the radicals of the 1860s, it is difficult to avoid a discussion of Bazarov's socio-historical prototypes. Let us stop for a moment, however, to consider the ambiguity inherent in the word "prototype." A colleague has suggested that a weakness in traditional literary scholarship is the failure to distinguish between "prototype" as a source of ideology, on the one hand, and as a personality model, on the other. Although such a neat distinction would no doubt facilitate precision in our discussion in this and preceding chapters, in practice it is difficult to place Bazarov's prototypes—literary and socio-historical—in one pigeonhole or the other. In attempting to maintain such a conceptual distinction, we are in effect asked to divorce content (ideology) from style (personality). Neither in literature nor in life is that easily accomplished, and as will be apparent from the subsequent discussion, all the possible prototypes who are about to be catalogued could serve as sources of both Bazarov's thoughts and his actions.

Conjectures about his prototypes began even before *Fathers and Sons* was published. The editorial board of *The Contemporary,* for instance, was certain that Turgenev's new novel was to be an attack on Dobroliubov.[6] The search for prototypes has continued into our time. In 1960 Batyuto proposed a new candidate—Lev Tolstoy.[7] Yury Mann has since made a noteworthy attempt to call a halt to these literary expeditions:

> Bazarov is not a photographic reproduction of anyone. It is time to stop comparing Bazarov to Chernyshevsky and Dobroliubov. The most that such comparisons can do is establish a certain similarity or difference, but they can hardly explain what Bazarov himself is about.[8]

Justified as Mann's exasperated sentiments are, there are nevertheless compelling reasons for reopening this thorny and much-abused investigation. It is foolhardy to pretend that Bazarov lacks prototypes: Turgenev was the first to admit that he always worked from a living model.[9] In addition, it is precisely on this question of Bazzarov's prototypes that the existing secondary material is most expansive and least reliable.

Let us make clear at the outset that Bazarov lacks any single prototype: he has many. Strakhov was the first to observe this: "Bazarov has many traits of people with whom we are acquainted. If no one preaches his whole system, we have heard the ideas expressed separately, fragmentarily, in a disjoined, incoherent way."[10]

According to various sources, Turgenev, in private coversations, named a small army of prototypes for Bazarov. Polovtsev recalls that Turgenev mentioned a certain Doctor Dmitriev.[11] Polovtsev's testimony, never corroborated by Turgenev or any other witnesses, has by now become a cliché of Turgenev criticism. Isaiah Berlin, Granjard, the editors of the Academy Edition of Turgenev's works, and others all state nonchalantly that Bazarov is based in part on Doctor Dmitriev.[12] This "fact" deserves to be viewed with more than a little scepticism: it represents hearsay, not conclusive evidence.[13] It is based on recollections, and human memory is notoriously inaccurate. Other memoirists mention a young doctor whom Turgenev allegedly met while travelling through Germany; still others mention a young doctor whom he supposedly encountered on a Russian train.[14] Ostrovskaia claims that Turgenev told her that Bazarov was based on the character of a young man with whom he became acquainted on the train and who was subsequently exiled to Siberia.[15] Her memoirs led to an article by Chernov in which the critic argued that this young man was probably Viktor Yakushkin.[16] William Edgerton, however, has since demonstrated conclusively that Chernov's hypothesis cannot be correct.[17] Berlin and Granjard both assert that one of Bazarov's models was a doctor whom Turgenev met on the Isle of Wight.[18] This claim seems to be the result of a misreading of the article "Apropos of *Fathers and Sons*," in which Turgenev writes:

> I was sea-bathing at Ventnor, a small town on the Isle of Wight—it was in August, 1860—when the first idea occurred to me of *Fathers and Sons,* the novel which deprived me, forever, I believe, of the good opinion of the Russian younger generation. I have heard it said and read it in critical articles not once but many times that in my works I always "started with an idea" or "developed an idea." Some people praised me for it, others, on the contrary, censured me; for my part, I must confess that I never attempted "to create a character" unless I had for my departing point not an idea but a living person to whom the appropriate elements were later on gradually attached and added. Not possessing a great amount of free inventive powers, I always felt the need of some firm ground on which I could plant my feet. The same thing happened with *Fathers and Sons;* at the basis of its chief character, Bazarov, lay the personality of a young provincial doctor I had been greatly struck by. (He died shortly before 1860.) In that remarkable man I could watch the embodiment of that principle which had scarcely come to life but was just beginning to stir at the time, the principle which later received the name of nihilism. Though very powerful, the impression that man left on me was still rather vague. At first I could not quite make him out myself, and I kept observing and listening to everything around me, as though wishing to check the truth of my own impressions. I was worried by the following fact: in not one work of our literature did I ever find as much as a hint of what I seemed to see everywhere; I could not help wondering whether I was not chasing after a phantom. On the Isle of Wight, I remember, there lived with me at the time a Russian who was endowed with excellent taste and a remarkable "nose" for everything which the late Apollon Grigoriev called "the ideas" of an epoch. I told him what I was thinking of and was astonishing to hear the following remark: "Haven't you created such a character already—in Rudin?" I said nothing. Rudin and Bazarov—one and the same character! (XII, 97-98)[19]

Later on in the same article Turgenev adds:

> In depicting Bazarov's personality, I excluded everything artistic from the range of his sympathies, I made him express himself in harsh and unceremonious tones, not out of an absurd desire to insult the younger generation (!!!), but simply as a result of my observations of my acquaintance, Dr. D., and people like him. (XII, 100)[20]

It seems likely that both Berlin and Granjard take the word "acquaintance" to refer to the young Russian on the Isle of Wight with Turgenev. But everything in the text argues for identifying the epithet with Dr. D., not with Turgenev's island acquaintance. The Russian acquaintance is specifically characterized as a man of excellent taste—a claim Turgenev neither would nor could have made for any of the nihilistic young men of the 1860s. Furthermore, in a letter to E. E. Lambert, dated August 6/18, 1860, Turgenev wrote from the Isle of Wight: "There are many Russians here—and good ones, among others N. Ya. Rostovtsev (the son of the famous Yakov Ivanovich)—an excellent person. I would be very glad if the two of you could meet some time" (4, 116). It seems likely that this is the acquaintance Turgenev describes in "Apropos of *Fathers and Sons.*"

It is important to note that the above-quoted passages contain the only statements about Bazarov's prototype that come directly from Turgenev. All the Dmitrievs, Siberian exiles, and others come to us second-hand and should be approached with extreme caution. We should insist, however, that even Turgenev's statement be taken with a larger-than-usual grain of salt, since he made so many contradictory statements about *Fathers and Sons* that in the last analysis it is difficult to believe anything that he said about it.

Belinsky is occasionally suggested as a prototype for Bazarov —though only rarely by Soviet commentators.[21] There are perhaps two major reasons for Soviet scholars' prevailing reluctance to consider Belinsky a prototype. The first is the widespread assumption that Bazarov's prototypes are the "new people" of the 1860s. As noted in Chapter III, not all Bazarov's prototypes are men of the 1860s: some of them, for instance, are types from Western European and earlier Russian literature. Second, implicit in much Turgenev criticism is the notion that the author was ultimately antagonistic toward his hero, just as he was toward many of the real-life men of the 1860s. Therefore, how could Belinsky, the great friend of Turgenev's youth, be the prototype for a hero towards whom Turgenev feels antipathy? One answer is that although Turgenev may have thought his hero totally misguided about life, he still was able to consider Bazarov a great tragic hero who was not lacking in admirable traits.

There is good reason for viewing Belinsky as one of Bazarov's prototypes. As Berlin points out, "Bazarov has some of Belinsky's characteristics—brusqueness, directness, intolerance."[22] (Dobroliubov and Chernyshevsky were, if anything, *more* brusque, direct, and intolerant than Belinsky.) There are certain passages in Turgenev's "Reminiscences of Belinsky" that invite comparison with Bazarov's portrait. Turgenev recalls that Belinsky did not know foreign languages (XIV, 27); neither does Bazarov.[23] Discussing Belinsky's ancestry, Turgenev recalls:

> His accent, manners, and gestures reminded one distinctly of his origins: his whole demeanor was typically Russian: one could immediately recognize a Muscovite in him; it was not for nothing that the blood flowing in his veins was pure and unadulterated—belonging as it did to the Great Russian priesthood which was for so many centuries impervious to the influence of any foreign race. (XIV, 26-27)

Significantly, Bazarov's essential Russianness is everywhere underscored in *Fathers and Sons,* especially in his speech. He prides himself on being of the people, attacks Pavel for using foreign words, and salts his own language with folksy phraseology.[24]

Characterizing Belinsky's personality, Turgenev notes that he was a man "devoted entirely to the truth, irritable but not egoistic, who knew how to love and hate disinterestedly" (XIV, 27). In the early chapters of *Fathers and Sons* Bazarov is similarly irritable and not entirely egoistic: he irks Pavel partly because his ego cannot be wounded by Pavel's barbs. Bazarov's self-esteem is not really at stake in the novel until the confrontation with Odintsova. Bazarov, like Belinsky in Turgenev's portrait, is "a good hater" (XIV, 53): in his conversation with Arkady (Ch. XXI) Bazarov expressed pride in his ability to hate (322-323).

Furthermore, according to Turgenev

> There was a large dose of intolerance in Belinsky. He did not admit, especially in the heat of an argument, a single drop of truth in his

> opponents' opinions and would turn away from them with the same sort of indignation with which he gave us his own opinions when he found them to be mistaken. (XIV, 53)

This is precisely Bazarov's manner in his arguments with Pavel, particularly in their major verbal battle in Chapter X, at the height of which Bazarov abruptly walks out on Pavel, dragging his disciple Arkady along with him.

There are also biographical parallels. Berlin points out, for instance, that Belinsky, like Bazarov, was the son of a poor army doctor.[25] Like Bazarov, he had an unsuccessful personal life. Turgenev recalls:

> I have reason to suspect that Belinsky, with his ardent and impressionable heart, with his affectionate and passionate nature, Belinsky, nevertheless one of the foremost people of his time, was never loved by a woman. His marriage was concluded for reasons other than passion. In his youth he had been in love with a certain noblewoman, the daughter of the landowner B[akuni]n of Tver; she was a poetic creature, but she loved another and anyway died soon. There also occurred in Belinsky's life a rather strange and sad romance with a girl of simple station; I remember his fragmentary, gloomy story about her... it produced a deep impression upon me... but it ended in nothing. (XIV, 56)

Lastly, there is the matter of the novel's being dedicated to Belinsky, a fact widely noted but little commented on. Surely the dedication must have had some special meaning for Turgenev, especially if we recall that *Fathers and Sons* is the only Turgenev novel to bear a dedication. Turgenev's own explanation of the dedication is bafflingly ambiguous. At the conclusion of a proposed preface to the novel's separate edition (after its original appearance in the journal *The Russian Herald*), Turgenev writes:

> I will limit myself to a couple of words: I myself know, and my friends are convinced of this, that my convictions have not changed even so much as a hair since my entry into the field of literature, and with a tranquil conscience I can set forth on the first page of this book the dear name of my unforgettable friend. (446)

But this leaves open at least two possible interpretations. Pustovoit asserts, for instance, that the dedication identifies Belinsky as the spiritual father of the men of the 1860s.[26] Therefore, by implication, the dedication indicates approval of the men of the 1860s and perhaps disapproval of the mediocre level to which men of the 1840s such as Pavel and Nikolay have sunk. On the other hand, although no one has suggested this possibility, it may be that Turgenev intended the dedication as an oblique reproach to the men of the 1860s, something along the lines of "Here's a real hero for you—a radical who also knew the value of art and civilization!" Such a reading is implied in Plekhanov's remarks about Turgenev and *The Contemporary:*

> Certain of "Belinsky's friends," who at first still considered that they could go along with Chernyshevsky and his confreres, broke off from *The Contemporary,* yelling that Belinsky would never have approved of the direction it had taken. This was the way I. S. Turgenev acted.[27]

This exegesis is further reinforced by Turgenev's remarks about Belinsky's negation (*otritsanie*—the same word that Bazarov uses): "Belinsky was as much an idealist as a negationist; he negated in the name of an ideal" (XIV, 42). This comment, made several years after the publication of *Fathers and Sons,* may have been intended as criticism of the new generation of negators who were devoid of ideals.

Perhaps, however, the dedication is best understood not as an evaluation of the ideologies and men of the 1840s and 1860s, but as a key to one of the novel's major themes—fate, in this particular instance the fate of the talented man in Russia. Freeborn suggests that Turgenev, having lost such close friends as Stankevich and Belinsky, came to the conclusion "that death is the law of fate, especially for those who try to dedicate themselves to Russia."[28] Bearing this in mind, we note that *Fathers and Sons* opens with a dedication of the novel to Belinsky's memory and closes with a sad celebration of Bazarov's memory. In this way the opening and closing chords of the novel echo a requiem perhaps not just for Belinsky and Bazarov, but also for Pushkin, Lermontov, Stankevich, Maykov, Dobroliubov, and all the other prodigiously talented young Russians whom Turgenev saw struck down during his lifetime.

Bazarov's most frequently adduced prototype is Dobroliubov. That there are links between Dobroliubov and Bazarov is fairly clear: it is the nature of these ties that remains problematical.

Various specialized studies have shown or tried to show that several of Bazarov's statement are nearly verbatim quotations from published works by Dobroliubov. Bazarov's dismissal of principles, authorities, and exposé literature in Chapter X is usually traced to Dobroliubov's "Last Year's Literary Trivia."[29] The parallels are there, to be sure, but Pisarev, in his "Scholasticism of the Nineteenth Century," is even more iconoclastic—and thus a more likely source for Bazarov's nihilism—than Dobroliubov.

Bazarov's notions about sensations (*oshchushcheniia*), i.e., that there are no principles, only sensations, and that sensations are the result of chemical reactions (325), are often traced to another Dobroliubov article, "Nikolay Vladimirovich Stankevich."[30] Here the parallels are forced, since Dobroliubov argues that people serve society because they get pleasure out of doing good,[31] that is, he expounds the ersatz enlightened self-interest typical of the era. According to that rather naive theory, by acting in his own interest, man not only secures hedonistic pleasure for himself but simultaneously contributes to the common good. Bazarov, on the other hand, propounds not enlightened self-interest, but a profoundly physiologico-deterministic view of the human personality. Bazarov and Dobroliubov are not speaking of the same things at all.

A long critical tradition exists according to which Dobroliubov's works cannot account for Bazarov's anti-esthetic views.[32] As Batyuto has recently demonstrated, however, Bazarov's statement that Pushkin was a military poet, that on every page he has "Into battle, into battle! For the honor of Russia!" (326), echoes a series of articles by Dobroliubov that includes "Pushkin's Works" and "V. Benediktov's New Poems," in which Dobroliubov upbraids Pushkin for his allegedly excessive respect for the bayonet and in which Dobroliubov generally turns Pushkin into a military poet.[33]

More convincing that any ideological kinship between Bazarov and Dobroliubov, however, are similarities in character and personality. Bazarov's brusqueness and intolerance are closer to Dobroliubov's than to Belinsky's. Bazarov's seeming lack of militancy, his laconic indifference to Pavel and Nikolay (24), may well be a reflection of the silent treatment accorded Turgenev by Dobroliubov.[34]

Lampert notes of Dobroliubov that "he is fairly typical of those whose rejection of error is more convincing and more meaningful than the positive formula in which they try to define what they believe."[35] That is another temperamental similarity between Bazarov and Dobroliubov, while on the social level they are linked by the fact that both are *raznochintsy*.

If we accept the premise that Bazarov is in some ways a variation on Dobroliubov, we are still left with defining the nature of the relationship between Dobroliubov and Turgenev's portrayal of Bazarov. Is it flattering, unflattering, a caricature? Turgenev always and everywhere denied that he had caricatured Dobroliubov in *Fathers and Sons*. His statement in "Apropos of *Fathers and Sons*" is typical:

> My critics described the novel as a "lampoon" and talked of my "exasperated" and "wounded" vanity; but why should I write a lampoon on Dobroliubov, whom I hardly met, but of whom I thought highly as a man and as a talented writer? (XIV, 99)

One must agree that Bazarov does not resemble a lampoon figure: on occasion his behavior may appear silly, his views naive and inconsistent, but he remains on the whole a commanding, tragic presence. Nonetheless, Turgenev's defense typically falls a little short of the truth. There is overwhelming evidence that Turgenev had little use for Dobroliubov.[36] Turgenev's remarks are a characteristic example of the tangled web of truths, half-truths, and untruths that he managed to spin around *Fathers and Sons*. It is fairly certain that he took pains here to write sympathetically of Dobroliubov because of the latter's tragic, early death (from tuberculosis)—a circumstance that would undoubtedly lead Turgenev's contemporaries to view remarks critical of Dobroliubov as the height of tactlessness.

That Bazarov was not conceived as a parody of Dobroliubov in no way diminishes the possibility that Turgenev planned Bazarov as an exposé. It is beyond question that the initial impulse for writing *Fathers and Sons* came out of Turgenev's break with *The Contemporary*: the atmosphere of the novel reeks of that breach. Chernyshevsky went so far as to call *Fathers and Sons* "an open declaration of Turgenev's hatred for Dobroliubov."[37] Chernyshevsky's reading of the novel is surely a misreading: what writer (other than Dostoevsky) would portray his enemy as a tragic, heroic figure? Yet the possibility remains that Turgenev began his novel as an exposé of Dobroliubov (and his kind), but that he moved far beyond an exposé pure and simple as he became progressively more attracted—albeit ambivalently so—to his hero.

Another figure frequently mentioned as a prototype is Chernyshevsky—largely because many of Bazarov's views and statements can be traced directly to works and remarks of the martyr-critic. Chernyshevsky thought and taught that men were essentially alike, that their moral differences could be accounted for on the basis of biology or environment.[38] Bazarov parrots those views in his conversation with Odintsova in Chapter XVI: his remarks, beginning with the statement that people are like trees in a forest and ending with his assertion that if one corrects society, moral illnesses will disappear (277) are a paraphrase of sections of Chernyshevsky's "The Russian at the *Rendez-vous*."[39]

Bazarov's ideas on esthetics are also substantially Chernyshevsky's. When Bazarov explains to Odintsova that a picture is occasionally valuable because it can demonstrate concisely what would require several pages of print to explain (276), he echoes Chernyshevsky's *On the Esthetic Relations of Art to Reality*.[40] Not surprisingly, few Soviet critics suggest that Bazarov and Chernyshevsky's esthetic views have anything in common.

As with Dobroliubov, critics and scholars have traced various of Bazarov's remarks to Chernyshevsky. For instance, anti-aristocratic remarks made by Chernyshevsky to Herzen found their way into Bazarov's argument with Arkady over Pavel's aristocratic upbringing and bearing (226) and into his attack on Pavel for aristocratic principles that benefit no one (242).[41] Bazarov's farewell to Arkady ("Our dust will eat your eyes, out mud will dirty you . . ." [380]) recalls a passage from Chernyshevsky's "K. C. Carey's Politico-Economic Letters to the President of the United States of America": "He who is afraid to be covered by dust and get his boots dirtied should not take up public service (*obshchestvennaia deiatelnost'*)."

Soviet scholarship tends to draw a line, as it were, after Dobroliubov and Chernyshevsky before going on to other possible prototypes. Much Soviet criticism treats Bazarov not as a single character, but as two: the pre-Odintsova Bazarov and the "pessimistic" Bazarov of the latter part of the novel. The first Bazarov is laudable, admirable, and "typical"; the other Bazarov is somehow guilty, unacceptable, atypical, and a product of Turgenev's class limitations. So runs the standard Soviet analysis.[43] Whereas the haloed Bazarov is akin to the exemplary Chernyshevsky and

Dobroliubov, his lesser counterpart, with his anti-esthetic, antipopular, and defeatist attitudes, is often viewed as an adaptation of the less praiseworthy Pisarev and Nikolay Uspensky.[44]

According to Petrov, for example, Bazarov's vulgar materialism, distrust of the peasantry, and anti-estheticism are typical of the youth of the 1860s who sided with Pisarev.[45] The tradition that Pisarev's views are reflected in Bazarov's denial of art began with Piksanov.[46] As Batyuto has pointed out, however, Pisarev's career as a destroyer of esthetics did not even begin until after *Fathers and Sons* was written.[47] In addition, everyone seems either to have forgotten or ignored the fact that Pisarev, in his article "Bazarov," criticized Bazarov for his overly narrow esthetic views.[48] Pisarev is hardly an appropriate whipping boy for Bazarov's antiestheticism. The question of Bazarov's materialism is one over which seas of ink have been spilled, particularly by Soviet critics. Moser sums up the issue very neatly:

> The emphasis placed by these men [Moleschott, Vogt, Büchner] on the importance of physiology led them [the intelligentsia of the 1860s] to espouse and propogate doctrines of "physiological determinism," the idea that characteristics or capabilities of an individual or a race are so determined by physiology that nothing can be done to alter these characteristics or capabilities. Such doctrines as these lead Soviet philosophers to look upon Vogt, Moleschott, and Büchner with suspicion—the Soviets would like to think that man can be transformed through the manipulation of his social environment—and to tag them "vulgar materialists" as distinguished from "dialectical materialists."[49]

According to the standard Soviet line, Chernyshevsky and Dobroliubov propogated dialetical materialsm, while Pisarev's materialism was of the vulgar variety. Consequently, Petrov and others are eager to tie the "bad" Bazarov to Pisarev. (They all ignore the fact that Dobroliubov's "philosophy" resembles Pisarev's more than it does Chernyshevsky's.) Bazarov's views on body chemistry as the source of man's personality and actions (325) have their basis, of course, in physiological determinism, but Bazarov also argues that man can be transformed through the manipulation of his social environment: "If society is corrected, there will be no [moral] illnesses," he tells Odintsova (277). This is not the theory of a "vulgar" materialist: as we have already seen it is a restatement of Chernyshevsky. The whole question of the exact nature of Bazarov's materialism is ultimately of little importance—and interest, but it points up once again the extraordinary extent of the deception commonly practiced in Soviet Turgenev scholarship.

Another frequently adduced "negative" prototype is Nikolay Uspensky, to whom Bazarov is likened in his anti-Pushkin and pessimistic anti-*narod* moments.[50] The rationale behind linking Bazarov to Uspensky vis-à-vis Pushkin has its origins in a letter to Annenkov (January 7/19, 1861) in which Turgenev writes:

> Recently the humanity-hater Uspensky (Nikolay) came through and had dinner at my place. He too felt it his responsibility to scold Pushkin, assuring [me] that all Pushkin did in all his poems was cry, "To battle! To battle for Holy Rus'"! However, he does not completely approve of Dobroliubov. It seems to me for some reason that he will go insane. (4, 182)

It is obvious that Turgenev gave Uspensky's remarks about Pushkin to Bazarov (326). But, as Batyuto argues, the context of Turgenev's characterization of Uspensky shows that Turgenev had in mind others besides Uspensky who felt it necesssary to scold Pushkin ("He too [*I on*])—probably Dobroliubov, whose articles on Pushkin have already been mentioned. As for Uspensky's depression, loss of faith in the people *(narod)*, and moral disintegration (which, as we see, Turgenev predicted accurately, albeit splenetically), they did not occur until the mid-1870s, so that it is hardly accurate to call Uspensky a prototype for Bazarov in that connection. If anything, this is a case of life imitating art, not the reverse.

The last major entry on the prototype sweepstakes is very much a dark horse—Lev Tolstoy. Batyuto, in a fascinating, tightly reasoned article, argues that Bazarov's conduct is not unlike Tolstoy's impudent, brash behavior toward Turgenev.[51] He quotes Fet on the tortured relations between Turgenev and Tolstoy:

> From the very first moment I noticed in the young Tolstoy a spontaneous opposition to everything generally accepted in the field of opinions . . . And I was a witness of the despair to which Turgenev, seething and breathing heavily from an argument, was brought by Tolstoy's obviously restrained, but [therefore] all the more venomous objections.[52]

Annenkov and Panaev second these impressions, and Batyuto concludes that Bazarov's socio-political nihilist is *not* Tolstoy's, but that they do have a certain all-embracing philosophical nihilism in common.⁵³ (As we shall see presently, Bazarov's nihilism is precisly that—philosophical, rather than socio-political.) No Soviet or Western scholars have taken Batyuto's suggestions seriously, which is a little surprising. It would be very easy to supplement Batyuto's hypothesis by linking it to Lenin's articles which view Tolstoy as a *de facto* apostle of revolution.⁵⁴ Instead scholars up to this point have passed over Batyuto's article in embarrassed silence, or, like Pustovoit, reject Tolstoy as a prototype because Bazarov and Tolstoy are too far apart ideologically.⁵⁵ In order to properly evaluate Batyuto's article and Pustovoit's dismissal of it, we ought first to examine the questions of Bazarov's views and his nihilism.

The conventional Soviet treatment of Bazarov, his views, and the 1860s (see the standard works by Pustovoit, Byaly, Brodsky, Petrov, Brazhe, *et. al.*) suffers from a major misapprehension— namely, that Bazarov can be identified with an integrated system of ideas which are explicitly articulated in the novel. Petrov, for instance, marshals non-existent evidence in an attempt to convince readers that Bazarov's clearly contradictory remarks about the peasantry are not at all inconsistent.⁵⁶ Byaly argues that in spite of Bazarov's pessimistic frame of mind, the latter has not relinquished his (unspecified) goals at the end of the novel.⁵⁷ In another work Byaly strives to establish—textual evidence to the contrary—that Bazarov is not just a destroyer, but that he also has constructive plans for the future.⁵⁸ Brazhe would have us believe that Bazarov has a theory about the correct organization of society, with its basis in human labor.⁵⁹ Apropos of Bazarov's statement that nihilists "laugh at medicine as a whole and respect no one" (313), Pustovoit offers this astonishing commentary:

> Can a doctor laugh at medicine? The fact is that there are different kinds of medicine. Bazarov laughs at that medicine which is based either on a mechanistic or idealistic philosophy and is not far removed from reading coffee grounds to predict the future (phrenology, vitalism).⁶⁰

In the instances noted, the scholars have based their conclusions either on non-existent or hopelessly insubstantial textual evidence. All are sterling examples of the lengths to which many Soviet scholars will go in order to find, i.e., create, a coherent pattern in Bazarov's views. In all honesty it must be noted that it is not only Soviet critics who attribute to Bazarov a systematic worldview.

Strakhov speaks of the "whole system" of Bazarov's thought,[61] while Reeve suggests that Bazarov's "faith in the community of mankind isolates him from men."[62]

Recently even some Soviet scholars have been willing to admit that Bazarov lacks a clear system of beliefs.[63] Several factors account for the absence of logical unity in his views. On the one hand, it is possible, as is implicit in much of what Batyuto writes, that Turgenev consciously chose to have Bazarov mouth those of the younger generations's views which he, Turgenev, found most objectionable, and expound them in a manner bound to raise doubts about their validity.[64] This seems not unlikely, in spite of Turgenev's quite unbelievable claim that "with the exception of Bazarov's views on art," he "shared almost all of his [Bazarov's] convictions" (XII, 100). On the other hand, we must understand that, as Granjard suggests, the ideas of the men of the 1860s, which combined a mechanico-materialistic explanation of the world and human nature with the ethics of English utilitarianism, were in no sense original and the entire system was coherent only in the sense that all of its points were directed against the Tsarist regime.[65] Since Bazarov's nihilistic theories are nothing more than a reformulation of the already incoherent views of the radicals of the 1860s, his views cannot be other than contradictory. Furthermore, as we have noted earlier, far from all of Bazarov's prototypes are men of the 1860s.

What then can one say of Bazarov's so-called nihilism? The assumption in masses of critical literature is that Bazarov is a budding revolutionary who is ready to sacrifice his life for the good of the peasantry, and that this readiness for self-sacrifice and revolution is the real meaning of his nihilism. The source for this notion is a letter to K. K. Sluchevsky (April 14/26, 1862), in which Turenev declared: "If he [Bazarov] is called a nihilist, that should be read as revolutionary" (4, 387). But in fact Bazarov's nihilism is not political: it is, as Granjard says, the refusal to recognize *any* principles.[66] We can hardly speak of Bazarov's "cause" *(delo)*, as some scholars nonetheless do, because he does not posit one. Irving Howe observes that Bazarov's nihilism

> must be taken more as a symptom of political desperation than as a formal intellectual system. He is ready for life and cannot find it. He is a man of intense emotions, but without confidence in his capacity to realize them. Bazarov is a revolutionary personality, but without

revolutionary ideas or commitments.[67]

If we insist on seeing Bazarov as a revolutionary, then we must limit ourselves to observing that he is one of the original rebels without a cause, and that his status as a revolutionary sooner lends itself to analysis in terms of temperament than socio-political ideology. Bazarov's nihilism is really nothing more or less than primitive empiricism: he has no *a priori* beliefs. He rejects all ideas, theories, and notions, until he has tested them personally. As Dale Peterson suggests, "Bazarov fancies himself the total experimentalist, the complete dispassionate and detached 'scientific' mind."[68] Tolstoy's philosophical nihilism, with its pattern of testing and rejecting is the reverse of Bazarov's empiricism, which rejects, then tests. Nonetheless, there is a similarity between Bazarov's and Tolstoy's nihilism: they represent the polar extremes implicit in a worldview that denies the relevance of any human experience other than one's own. Batyuto's point has a certain validity. Drawing attention to Bazarov's nihilism as a philosophical stance helps us to see that there is an underlying consistency in Bazarov—one that is obscured by attempts to explain his nihilism in political or ideological terms. Bazarov is a changed person at the end of the novel, and consequently his views have changed, but he remains an empiricist to the end.[69]

Pavel and Nikolay, in various ways and to varying degrees, typify the nobility of the generation of the 1840s. Turgenev himself names his characters' protoypes:

> Countess Salias is wrong in saying that people like Nikolay Petrovich and Pavel Petrovich are our grandfathers: Nikolay Petrovich is me, Ogarev, and thousands of others; Pavel Petrovich is Stolypin, Esakov, Rosset, also our contemporaries. They are the best of the gentry . . . . (4, 380)

In identifying Nikolay with Ogarev, Turgenev no doubt has in mind Nikolay's reform-minded, perhaps even leftist sympathies, along with a thoroughgoing devotion to art. We recall that Nikolay has undertaken—largely unsuccessfully—so many reforms that his neighbors call him "red" (329). And as noted earlier, Nikolay's difficulties with the estate are very much Turgenev's own.[71] The prototypes whom Turgenev suggests for Pavel are all social lions and career officers, as was Pavel in his youth. In addition, Pavel is a combination Anglophile-Slavophile. He reads English novels and newspapers, dresses like an English aristocrat, and generally orients himself toward England.[72] Because of Pavel's defense of the aristocracy and his condemnation of violence, Granjard argues that he is Turgenev's ideological mouthpiece, that some of Pavel's statements are as much anti-Herzen as they are anti-*raznochintsy*.[73] Granjard singles out Pavel's tirade against brute force in this respect (246), and suggests that the Pavel-Bazarov debates are a hint of the later Turgenev-Herzen polemics.[74]

Pavel's Slavophilism is underlined in various ways: his defense of the Russian *narod* against what he perceives as Bazarov's attacks on it, his ashtray in the form of a bast shoe, and his belated interest in the Orthodox Church (400). His Slavophilism is subjected to a comic treatment: it parodies the views and interests of the Slavophiles of the 1840s.

The ultimate symbol of the social, ideological, and generational conflicts of the 1860s is Pavel and Bazarov's duel. But the question remains as to what precisely the duel as ideological confrontation means. Does it signify the defeat of the nobility, as Freeborn argues?[75] Or does it represent the triumph of "the old," as Howe maintains?[76] Turgenev, in a letter to Sluchevsky, gave this answer to the question:

> The duel with Pavel Petrovich was introduced as a visual demonstration of the emptiness of elegant gentry knighthood, it was portrayed almost exaggeratedly comically; and how could he [Bazarov] have refused; after all, Pavel Petrovich would have clubbed him. Bazarov, in my opinion, continually defeats *(ravbivaet)* Pavel Petrovich, and not the other way around. (4, 380)

Many scholars and critics do not share Turgenev's view of the duel, however. Howe points out:

> During the duel, it is true, Pavel Petrovich must yield to Bazarov, but the mere fact that it takes place is a triumph for the old, not the new. Bazarov may regard Pavel Petrovich as an "archaic phenomenon," but the "archaic phenomenon" retains social power.[77]

The very fact that Bazarov participates in the duel shows that he has been co-opted into the system he vehemently rejects. Bazarov himself as much as says that when he describes the duel to Arkady:

> "Yes, brother," he [Bazarov] said, "that's what it means to spend a while with feudal barons. You youself find yourself a feudal baron and participate in knightly tournaments." (370)

Furthermore, as Vinogradov notes, the duel is used to reveal the flimsiness *(nesostoiatelnost)* of Bazarov's theories.[78] He rejects all stereotyped conventions, yet submits to a duel. Given the chance to destroy "the old," to take another shot at Pavel, he suddenly backs away from the opportunity.

The question of the duel's meaning is only part of a larger issue—that of the author's attitude toward the conflicts portrayed in *Fathers and Sons*. As already noted, Turgenev avowed that he was an objective writer and assured Fet that there was no "tendency" in the novel. [79] But this is only one side of the story. At other times Turgenev admitted that his novel was not impartial. He wrote to Sluchevsky: "My entire *povest* is directed against the gentry as a progressive class. . . . They [Pavel and Nikolay] are the best of the gentry—and because of that chosen by me to prove their flimsiness *(nesostoiatelnost)*" (4, 380). Moreover, in "Apropos of *Fathers and Sons*," Turgenev wrote that he "oversalted" Pavel, "drew out his flaws almost to the point of caricature, made him laughable" (XII, 101).

Turgenev stopped short of ever claiming that his novel was not intended as an exposé of the radicals. He asserted on occasion that he found Bazarov an extraordinarily winning figure. In the letter to Sluchevsky cited earlier, Turgenev writes of his hero:

> Bazarov nonetheless overwhelms all the novel's other characters. . . . The qualities assigned to him are not accidental. I wanted to make him a tragic figure—there was no room for tenderness here. He is honest, upright, and a democrat to his fingertips—and you don't find *good* sides to him?" (4, 379)

In this same letter Turgenev adds:

> If the reader does not grow to love Bazarov, with all his coarseness, heartlessness, pitiless dryness, and sharpness—if he doesn't grow to love him, I repeat—then I am at fault and did not achieve my goal. (4, 381)

Regardless of Turgenev's intentions and protestations, his allegiance was divided half-heartedly between the novel's ideological and social opponents. Pavel is, of course, almost an absurd character whose empty lionizing, aristocratic "principles," and way of life are unambiguously rejected. But Nikolay and Arkady are not ridiculous. Nikolay's marriage to Fenechka demonstrates his fundamental decency, and Arkady's moderate success as an estate manager suggests that when it comes to alleviating the hard life of the peasantry, gradualism is more effective than Bazarov's rhetoric about his "cause." Nikolay and Arkady are not dramatic transformers of society, but their modest efforts yield more tangible results that does all of Bazarov's talk about negating.[80] At the conclusion of the novel we sense that Russia's future could be in better hands than those of Nikolay and Arkady, yet we hardly feel that all is lost. In fact, there are grounds for optimism.

In spite of Turgenev's claim that he shared almost all of Bazarov's views (XII, 101), Bazarov is portrayed in such a way that the reader cannot help but conclude that Bazarov's nihilism is a denial of life. In a letter to Katkov Turgenev admitted that his portrait of Bazarov was not entirely sympathetic:

> Odintsova should not be ironical [about Bazarov], nor should the peasant stand higher than Bazarov, even if he himself is empty and barren... Perhaps my view of Russia is more misanthropic than you suppppose: he is, in my eyes, really a hero of our time. "What a hero and what a time," you'll say... But that's the way it is. (4, 303)

(We ought not to dismiss the likelihood that Turgenev was trying to ingratiate himself with Katkov, who was anything but sympathetic to the radicals.) Elsewhere Turgenev wrote that he conceived of Bazarov as a figure "doomed to perish—because he nevertheless stands on the threshold of the future" (4, 381). Within the context of the novel, however, Bazarov is doomed not because he is a hero born out of time, but because his views do not stand up to the test of life. Bazarov's scornful rejection of human history is grand enough, but when put to the test it collapses—and the impotence of his negation is not at all a function of the age in which he lives. Bazarov's rage against the Russian society of his day is justified, but Turgenev suggests that Bazarov's nihilism is hardly the proper instrument for bettering Russia. Human beings are not trees in the forest, and there is more to love than physiology. Bazarov's crude empiricism is not healthy skepticism: as the novel demonstrates, it is the manifestation of a profoundly morbid mode of thought.

Thus, Turgenev seems to argue in his novel that both sides, the gentry of the 1840s and the *raznochintsy* of the 1860s, are right in some ways and wrong in others. The truth is on both sides, but neither side has an exclusive claim to it. In a letter to E. E. Lambert Turgenev writes: "Since the time of ancient tragedy we have known that the real conflicts are those in which both sides are to *a certain extent* right" (4, 262). Turgenev was speaking of the "Polish question," but his remarks have equal validity for *Fathers and Sons*. Turgenev does take a stand in *Fathers and Sons*, and it is ambivalent, but not contradictory. Moser calls it "a plague of both your houses" attitude,[81] but it must be admitted that Turgenev sees positive elements in both sides too. In other words, the nobility, with its reformism and commitment to civilization, and the radicals, with their rejection of reform and tradition, are equally right and equally wrong.

Thus, Turgenev's socio-political stance in *Fathers and Sons* dovetails with the dualistic view of life and human nature posited in the first chapter of the present monograph. The Kirsanovs and their wives are limited, but limitlessly happy and fruitful; Bazarov is dramatic, intense, and barren. The Kirsanovs' love of life is justified, as is Bazarov's rage against Russian society. Nikolay and Arkady's ability to deal with the social problems of their day is limited, but does not give cause for despair; Bazarov's disgust with the gentry and limited, gradual reform is justified, but his "solutions" are wrongheaded.

V

FATHERS AND SONS AND TURGENEV'S OEUVRE

D. S. Mirsky, writing about Turgenev, speaks for the majority of critics and the reading public at large when he says: "The best of the novels and ultimately the most important of Turgenev's works is *Fathers and Sons,* one of the greatest novels of the nineteenth century."[1] A comparison of *Fathers and Sons* with Turgenev's other works—particularly the novels—reveals as well that it is in many ways atypical. Generalizations made about Turgenev's *oeuvre* often turn out to be inaccurate if one attempts to apply them to *Fathers and Sons.* It is likely that these two phenomena are not unrelated: the position of *Fathers and Sons* as Turgenev's best (and most popular) novel is a function of its atypicality.

Mirsky suggests that one of the reasons *Fathers and Sons* is so good is that in it Turgenev solved a problem that had long been plaguing him, i.e., "the contradiction between the imaginative and the social theme."[2] Turgenev's resolution of that dichotomy is multi-faceted, but essentially it involves fusing a love story (Turgenev's primary imaginative theme) and social observation into an organic whole. On the formal level, this means integrating the *povest* and the novel.

Turgenev's *povesti,* to quote Fisher, are interesting because they are "the product of the writer's pure inspiration, without any pretense of raising social issues."[3] What this means in more concrete terms is that most of the *povesti* are love stories without publicistic overtones. As Kagan-Kans notes, the spotlight in Turgenev's *povesti* falls on "the protagonist's inner life, his love and death. . . ."[4] Many of the *povesti* share a common accent on disillusionment, regrets, and loneliness of a man who has been destroyed either by love, or conversely, an inability to love. In such works as "Faust," "A Journey into the Woodlands," and "Asya," these themes are especially predominant.[5]

In the novels, on the other hand, Turgenev responds to Belinsky's demand for an *engagé* literature. In Mirsky's formulation, "The novels of Turgenev are, thus, those of his stories in which he, voluntarily, submitted to the obligation of writing works of social significance."⁶ It is of note that Mirsky's remark implies a kinship between the *povesti* and the novels, i.e., the central role of a love story in both genres. Turgenev's task in the novels, then, was to combine the love stories with social comment—a task at which he was often proved inept.

It is a cliché of Turgenev criticism that Turgenev's novels are surrounded by clusters of *povesti* which are related thematically to the novels and sometimes serve as preparatory sketches for them.⁷ Batyuto has recently subjected this cliche to healthy scrutiny:

> Thus, for instance, the generally-accepted opinion that Turgenev's novel is usually surrounded by a "ring" of *povesti,* which are in a way preparatory etudes for it, is true, but extremely imprecise. Such a conclusion can be applied completely to *Rudin* and *A Nest of Gentlefolk.* Applied to the novels *On the Eve* and *Virgin Soil,* it clearly needs substantial qualifications and limitations, and in regard to the novel *Fathers and Sons,* it is perhaps completely untrue. In point of fact, the identification of a "ring" of *povesti*-etudes that are directly preparatory for this novel is very, very difficult.⁸

The problem with Batyuto's analysis is that he provides no criteria for distinguishing directly preparatory sketches from indirectly preparatory ones. He mentions neither "Yakov Pasynkov" nor "Hamlet and Don Quixote," which, as noted earlier, are preliminary materials for *Fathers and Sons.* He does cite similarities between Pavel and the father in "First Love,"⁹ and as Kagan-Kans has shown, it is equally possible to demonstrate ties between Bazarov and the father.¹⁰

After rejecting the notion that there are directly preparatory *povesti* for *Fathers and Sons,* Batyuto goes on to link the inserted novella *(vstavnaia novella)* in Chapter VII, which relates Pavel's pre-history, to one of Turgenev's earlier *povesti,* "A Correspondence," which dates from 1855-1856.¹¹ He establishes the connection by tracing the heroines of "A Correpondence" and the inserted novella to a single prototype, Pauline Viardot. Thus Batyuto implies that the inserted novella has something in common with Turgenev's *povesti.* Byaly suggests the same thing when he argues that Pavel's pre-history, "because of its style and tone, its general character, seems to *(kak by)* drop out of the context of *Fathers and Sons."* He perceives in it the contours of a romantic novella.¹² But both Batyuto and Byaly fail to draw what seems an obvious conclusion: Pavel's pre-history is in fact a condensed Turgenev *povest*, and on the formal level Turgenev combines personal vision and social comment (a contradiction reflected in the division of his works into *povesti* and novels) by introducing the *povest* into the very texture of *Fathers and Sons*.

What justification is there for calling the inserted novella a *povest* in the Turgenevian sense of the word? It resembles a *povest* in several ways. Kagan-Kans notes that many of the *povesti* contain an autobiographical element.[13] Pavel's pre-history clearly manifests such an element: the motif of a young man's abandoning his career and wandering through Europe in pursuit of a woman who loves him only intermittently cannot fail to call to mind Turgenev's relations with Pauline Viardot. In addition, like the *povesti*, Pavel's pre-history has no socio-political overtones—it is purely the story of a love and its consequences. And the fact that the pre-history centers around a love and its *disastrous* consequences sets the novella off from the other pre-histories in *Fathers and Sons*. The compositional pattern of a love confrontattion that destroys the hero emotionally and leaves him only bittersweet memories for a lonely old age brings the inserted novella close to such *povesti* as "Faust," "Yakov Pasynkov," and "First Love," among others. Though it lacks the first-person narration typical of the *povest*,[14] it is in all other respects a quintessential, albeit condensed Turgenev *povest*.

Pavel's pre-history resembles many of Turgenev's *povesti* both in form and function. Just as the *povesti* around *Rudin* and *A Nest of Gentlefolk* serve as preparatory sketches for and illuminate those novels, so Pavel's pre-history sounds the major theme of *Fathers and Sons*—love and fate in the lives of young gentlemen of analogous temperament and similarly great expectations.

The inclusion of a *povest* in the novel is merely formal evidence of the major trait that sets *Fathers and Sons* off from Turgenev's other novels, namely, the interpenetration of the love story and the social theme. We should add that the social theme is so well integrated into the novel's thematics that a contemporary reader can read *Fathers and Sons* without suspecting that there is a topical side of the novel which is escaping him. He will perceive the work as a study of clashes in temperament, because in *Fathers and Sons* the generational, social, and ideological conflicts of the 1860s are transmuted into collisions of personality types.

The commingling of a love story and social theme occurs on several levels. In the first place, *Fathers and Sons* contains not just a single love story involving a central hero and/or heroine, but multiple love relationships. No other Turgenev novel can claim this. This mushrooming of love intrigues both implies and is a function of an expanded view of society. By depicting numerous amorous entanglements Turgenev inevitably draws attention away from the central hero toward his milieu: thus in *Fathers and Sons* we see a larger segment of Russian society than that to which we are exposed in earlier Turgenev novels.[15] Thus, the intimate theme and social comment are organically linked. Additionally, and more significantly, the love stories of the sons can be fully appreciated and understood only when compared to those of the fathers. Bazarov's confrontation with Odintsova acquires added significance because of its echoes of Pavel's pre-history. Arkady's romance with Katya, when it is compared with his father's first marriage, reveals the similarity of the worldview espoused by father and son. When contrasted to Nikolay's romance with Fenechka, it reveals that the father is perhaps more "socially progressive" than his reform-minded son. Thus the social theme of the generation conflict and the personal love theme are inextricably joined. Furthermore, Bazarov's rationalist notions about life and love are shattered by his revelatory experience with Odintsova. Here is yet another way in which the social theme—in this case nihilism as an ideology—is illuminated by the love theme. In most of Turgenev's novels a genuine merging of the love theme and the social themes is absent. The experiences in love of Lavretsky *(A Nest of Gentlefolk),* Insarov *(On the Eve),* and Litvinov *(Smoke)* have nothing whatsoever to do with those novels' social concerns. Nezhdanov's inability to love in *Virgin Soil* is a symptom of his own spiritual bankruptcy, but it is in no way a comment on Populism, the major social theme of the novel. Only in *Rudin* does Turgenev manage to interweave sociology and love almost as successfully as in *Fathers and Sons.* Rudin's inability to give himself to Natalia is treated as a glaring example of his larger inability to translate his words into deeds. In the figure of Rudin the whole generation of glorious talkers of the 1840s is implicitly condemned. (One of the conclusions to be drawn here is that of all Turgenev's heroes, only Rudin and Bazarov are truly heroes of their time. They not only mouth the social and philosophical concerns of their age [as do Insarov and Nezhdanov], but their very characters embody the spirit of the age they represent.)

Gippius observes of Turgenev's works that "the more organically linked the novel's psychological intrigue is to its socio-ideological tasks, the more shapely *(stroinee)* is its composition."[16] It is because of this harmonious blending of "psychological intrigue" with its "socio-ideological tasks" that Mirsky calls *Fathers and Sons* "Turgenev's only novel where the social problem is distilled without residue into art, and leaves no bits of undigested journalism sticking out."[17]

An important aspect of the distillation of the social problem into art is the use of dialogue in the novel. As noted in the first chapter on characterization, dialogue in *Fathers and Sons,* whether it revolves around personal matters or social issues, is always used for purposes of characterization.[18] Such is not always the case in Turgenev's other novels—particularly in *Smoke* and *Virgin Soil,* where dialogue often degenerates into unconcealed didacticism divorced from characterization. The distasteful sententiousness of these later novels may well stem from the fact that Turgenev's draft plans for them included thesis statements, guidelines which he did not formulate for the first four novels.[19] At any rate, in these last novels—especially in *Smoke*—the publicistic passages become increasingly obtrusive, the dialogue less and less revelatory of character, and the accompanying stories more and more irrelevant to the social issues under discussion.

The intimate and social themes in *Fathers and Sons* are linked not only by dialogue, but by nature descriptions as well. When Arkady views the family estate through the eyes of a nihilist, he sees only poverty and decrepitude (205). When he sinks into thought, however, "spring takes its own," and Arkady succumbs to the beauty surrounding him (205-206). Here Turgenev uses two contrasting landscapes to illustrate opposing worldviews— that of the nihilist and the "older generation," of which Arkady is in fact a representative. Later in the novel another landscape serves a similarly dual purpose. Nikolay, sitting alone in his garden, asks himself: "But to reject poetry? . . . Not to have sympathy for art, nature?..." (249). Therein follows a lyrical nature description which both characterizes Nikolay and casts doubts on the essential wisdom of Bazarov's rejection of nature, an integral part of his nihilism. In all of Turgenev's novels, the responses of his characters to nature serve as a moral touchstone. As a general rule positive types respond to nature, negative ones do not. Only in

Fathers and Sons, however, are Turgenev's landscapes infused with social significance in addition to functioning as barometers of mood and temperament.

It was mentioned earlier that *Fathers and Sons* is an atypical Turgenev novel in that it does not treat the history of a single hero or heroine's passion, but describes multiple entanglements. Freeborn catalogues some of them: Nikolay and Fenechka, Pavel and Fenechka, Bazarov and Odintsova, and Arkady and Katya.[20] One could add several more: Nikolay and his first wife, Pavel and Princess R., Bazarov and Fenechka. The novel also features several stillborn affairs: Bazarov and Dunyasha (237, 358), Arkady and Odintsova, Odinstova and her Swede (283). One could argue in addition that Arkady and Bazarov's aborted friendship is a nonerotic variation on the love story.

Kagan-Kans points out that Turgenev's early works offer only two views of love: love as bourgeois happiness, which is equated with *poshlost* ("Andrey Kolosov," "Two Friends"), and love as a mortal illness ("First Love," "Faust," "Country Doctor").[21] In fact, however, this "either-or" seems to be the basis for any number of Turgenev's works, but in *Fathers and Sons* Turgenev moves beyond this dichromatic scheme to portray a wide variety of loves, many of which are neither lethal nor pathetically limited. For Pavel and Bazarov love is definitely a spiritual disease, but in describing Nikolay and his first and second wives, and Arkady and Katya, Turgenev portrays love as a balm for the spirit.[23] In Bazarov's interviews with Fenechka erotic interest takes the form of flirtation. Bazarov's parents offer a portrait of marital love as touching dedication and mutual support. In short, in *Fathers and Sons* love is perceived not only as passionate and destructive, but idyllic and constructive as well. Here we should note that Freeborn's generalization that love relationships in Turgenev never arise between similar types, while generally true, cannot be applied to *Fathers and Sons.*[24] In fact, many of the unions in *Fathers and Sons* are between people who are akin in temperament and social estate. Consider, for instance, Arkady and Katya, Nikolay and his first wife, and Bazarov's parents.

The major love story in *Fathers and Sons,* that involving Bazarov and Odintsova, differs quantitatively and qualitatively from the romances in Turgenev's other novels. As Pustovoit notes, the Bazarov-Odintsova intrigue, which is treated in Chapters XIV-XVIII, is condensed more than usual in Turgenev.[25] Surely this is what Fridlender and Batyuto have in mind when they suggest that Bazarov's involvement with Odintsova is not as important as similar confrontations in the earlier novels.[26] It is difficult to believe that they mean to say that the love confrontation is any less crucial than in other works: it is not, but its role as a plot element is vastly reduced.

One result of the contracted love story is that *Fathers and Sons* lacks a central heroine, and as Boyd points out, for that reason it is unique among Turgenev's novels.[27] *Fathers and Sons* has two heroines, Katya and Odintsova, neither of them really central. Other Turgenev novels have pairs of heroines *(Nest of Gentlefolk, Smoke)*, but *Fathers and Sons* is significantly different because in those novels the central heroes, Lavretsky and Litvinov, are torn between the two heroines. Such is not the case with *Fathers and Sons,* where it is Arkady, not Bazarov, who must choose between the two heroines. (In the first chapter it was suggested that *Fathers and Sons* has two heroes—one comedic, Arkady, and one tragedic, Bazarov. That Arkady's story line revolves around two contrasting heroines, thus paralleling a similar compositional technique in *Nest of Gentlefolk* and *Smoke,* is additional formal evidence that within Turgenev's novelistic world Arkady is more than a secondary hero.)

As the female protagonist, Odintsova is unique within Turgenev's *oeuvre.* She is not quite a central heroine: she does not fit into either of the two categories into which Turgenev's heroines seem to fall. One such category is comprised of "Turgenev maidens" *(turgenevskie devushki)*, models of virtuous Russian womanhood, strong (if at times shy) creatures who seem more committed to ideas and ideals than to people. Natalia *(Rudin)*, Liza *(Nest of Gentlefolk)*, Elena *(On the Eve)*, Tanya *(Smoke)*, and Marianna *(Virgin Soil)* are all "Turgenev maidens" in full flush. Mirsky notes of such heroines:

> His [Turgenev's] heroines are famous all the world over and have done much to spread a high reputation of Russian womanhood. Moral force and courage are the keynote to Turgenev's heroine—the power to sacrifice all worldly considerations to passion . . . or all happiness to duty . . . .[28]

Odintsova is not such a heroine, nor is Katya. Byaly notes that there is no "Turgenev maiden" to judge the hero in *Fathers and*

Sons.[29] The absence of "Turgenev maidens" in the novel may well be a point in its favor. Of all the women in the novel, Katya is closest to a "Turgenev maiden," but she lacks their awesome moral strength, and as Boyd notes, she is unlike previous heroines in that she is devoted to people, not to ideas.[30] And unlike the typical "Turgenev maiden," who, as Kagan-Kans writes, "tends not to be very clever,"[31] Katya is perceptive, even shrewd.

The second general category of Turgenev females includes the infernal women, the vampires, the heroines who consciously manipulate and attempt to destroy the men with whom they come into contact. Examples of such woman are Varvara *(Nest of Gentlefolk)*, Irina *(Smoke)*, and Sipyagina *(Virgin Soil)*. Odintsova is distinctly unlike Varvara in that she is not morally depraved. Nor does she have much in common with Sipyagina, the most consciously manipulative of Turgenev's heroines. If Odintsova resembles any of these infernal women, it is Irina, who invites the hero to commit himself but then withdraws at the decisive moment. Irina, however, is clearly a passionate creature, and her passion is destructive both to herself and to others. Odintsova, however, is neither depraved nor passionate, nor overtly manipulative. She, like Bazarov, is an enigmatic character, of whom there are very few in Turgenev's schematically-organized novelistic world.

Just as Odintsova and Katya are atypical Turgenev heroines in terms of character and compositional role, so is Bazarov an exception within Turgenev's gallery of heroes. Mirsky has called him "the only one of Turgenev's men worthy to stand by the side of his women."[32] On the formal level, as we have noted in other connections, Bazarov is atypical in his complete lack of a pre-history. Insarov *(On the Eve)* and Nezhdanov *(Virgin Soil)*, Turgenev's other hero-revolutionaries, have sketchy biographies, but Bazarov has no pre-history at all. In terms of composition, Bazarov is an exception in that unlike Lavretsky or Litvinov, he does not stand between two contrasting heroines (unless one pretends that his relations with Fenechka are anything more than meaningless flirtation), nor, as in the case of Rudin, Insarov, and Nezhdanov, is his sole involvement with a "Turgenev maiden." The mold is broken. In addition, Bazarov's character distinguishes him from other Turgenev heroes. He is not the passive plaything of machinating women that Lavretsky and Litvinov are. He does not suffer from Rudin's and Nezhdanov's inability to commit themselves. He does not share Insarov's simplistic simplemindedness, and in contrast to the latter wooden hero, Bazarov is made of flesh and blood. He is both strong and weak, admirable and pitiable, certain and doubting. All the other Turgenev heroes seem infinitely shallow and schematic when compared to Bazarov. Moreover, other Turgenev heroes are either incapable of love (Rudin, Nezhdanov) or they manifest a love that is strongly poeticized. Many of Turgenev's enamoured couples seem to live in a sexless world, even when we know that their love has been consummated, as in the case of Litvinov and Irina. Bazarov is once again an exception. He is capable of profound feeling, and Turgenev's portrait of Bazarov in love reveals not only a love poetically conceived ("And now here you stand, so beautiful..." the dying Bazarov tells Odintsova [395]), but one that is at the same time elemental in its passion. Note the description of Bazarov just after he has made his declaration of love:

> Odintsova extended both her arms, but Bazarov leaned his forehead against the windowpane. He was breathing heavily; his entire body was trembling obviously. But this was not the trembling of youthful shyness, not the sweet horror of a first declaration that had overcome him: this was passion burning in him, strong and oppressive *(tiazhelaia)* —passion which resembles spite *(zloba)* and is perhaps related to it.... (299)

Odintsova, recalling the scene, "sank in thought and flushed, recalling Bazarov's almost bestial face when he rushed at her" (300). Bazarov is Turgenev's only truly passionate hero, and, in the last analysis, his passionate nature is one of the major traits that so sets him off from other Turgenev heroes.

Another phenomenon that makes Bazarov an unusual Turgenev hero is the fact that in *Fathers and Sons* we not only see the hero's character revealed, but we observe its development as well. In this respect Bazarov is Turgenev's only dynamic hero.[33]

It has been observed earlier that the composition of *Fathers and Sons* is remarkable for a Turgenev novel. Gippius' classic Formalist work on the composition of Turgenev's novels affords ample support for such a contention. According to Gippius, "All six novels have a clear, essential similarity. In the center of each stand a hero and heroine plus three characters who are arrayed in fixed relations to the hero."[34] One of the people around him, from a lower social order and a lower ideological plane, is a rival for the heroine. A second character, who may also be a rival for the heroine, is hostile to the hero and is his ideological antipode. The third character is the hero's ideological confederate, or is at least a person from the same ideological milieu.[35] If we apply this scheme to *Fathers and Sons,* several problems become apparent. Bazarov and Odintsova do not really stand at the core of the novel: Bazarov does, but Odintsova does not. Moreover, only two of the usual three male characters flank the hero. Pavel represents the second category, the ideological antipode, and Arkady the third, but the first category goes unrepresented in *Fathers and Sons.* In addition, we note that Arkady, the rival for the heroine, comes not from the first category—someone from a lower social and ideological plane—but from the third category. As suggested earlier, Arkady is nearly as central a hero in the work as Bazarov. His function in the novel is not simply that of a rival for the heroine, but he also carries along the comedic plot line, in which Bazarov is a peripheral figure.

Gippius goes on to say that secondary characters—male and female—also fit into those categories that he sets up for primary characters. Thus, Nikolay, Bazarov's rival for Fenechka, fits the first category; Bazarov's father, his ideological antipode, the second; and Sitnikov the third.[36] Gippius himself admits that his scheme does not quite work for the secondary female characters in *Fathers and Sons,* because there are "too many" females in the novel.[37] Gippius' work thus reveals that the compositional pattern in *Fathers and Sons* is atypical for Turgenev, and, in addition, offers a prime example of generalizations about Turgenev which can accommodate *Fathers and Sons* only by stretching things more than a little.

Additional evidence that *Fathers and Sons* differs from Turgenev's other novels in compositional technique is offered in recent articles by Virginia Burns and Alexander Fischler.[38] Conventional wisdom insists that Turgenev's works (along with those of most other Russian authors) are plotless. Burns subjects *Fathers and Sons* to a rigorous structural analysis, charting contours of intrigue and tension in the novel. She concludes that *Fathers and Sons* is a highly-plotted work and that this emphasis on plot sets the novel off from Turgenev's other narratives.[39] Fischler seconds this notion:

> The *manque d'architecture* in his works, which Turgenev confessed, is

at the most an apology for frequent reliance on structural devices and conventions. Obviously, it did not always serve him well, but obviously also, *Fathers and Sons* is a notable exception: here, the uneasy coexistence of the old and the new, the artificial and the "natural" was in perfect accord with the main themes the author had chosen.[40]

What has been demonstrated in this chapter is that in matters of characterization, composition, and thematic concerns, *Fathers and Sons* is significantly different from Turgenev's other works. In the next chapter we will take up the contrasting question of what things *Fathers and Sons* has in common with the Russian classics that preceded it and followed it.

VI

FATHERS AND SONS:
A QUINTESSENTIAL RUSSIAN NOVEL

It is often remarked of Pushkin that all the currents of the eighteenth century converge in his works, out of which, in turn, arise the major trends of the nineteenth century. The position that *Fathers and Sons* holds in Russian literature is analogous in the sense that its sources are Pushkinian, Lermontovian, and Gogolian, while its implications are Dostoevskian and Tolstoyan. Although Turgenev's masterpiece is often studied as a documentary record of the ideological struggle among the intelligentsia of the 1860s, the novel is perhaps more important for literary history because of the central place it occupies in the evolution of the Russian novel. In his finest novel Turgenev draws on and sums up the themes, styles, and techniques of his most notable predecessors, while simultaneously orienting the reading sometimes tentatively, sometimes boldly, in the directions that the Russian novel will take in the hands of his contemporaries and successors.

Fathers and Sons is studded with direct and indirect allusions to Pushkin and his works: Nikolay quotes *Evgeny Onegin* (206); he reads his beloved "The Gypsies" (239); Arkady and Bazarov quarrel about Pushkin (325-326); and the last lines of the novel contain a hidden reference to Pushkin's "When I wander along the noisy streets" (*Brozhu li ia vdol ulits shumnykh*).[1] Whether these references are conscious or unconscious efforts on Turgenev's part to remind us of the Pushkinian sources for his novel is impossible to ascertain. Even without them, however, we would have no difficulty identifying the Pushkin heritage in *Fathers and Son.*

Fathers and Sons is Pushkinian first of all in that like *Evgeny Onegin*, it is a hero-centered work. Without its central hero there would be no novel. More importantly, the hero is a representative of his age, a hero of his time, and the novel as a whole is a kind of assessment of the period in which he lives. Pumpiansky provides a handy generic pigeonhole for this sort of novel: he calls it "culture-heroed" *(kulturno-geroichesky)* and identifies *Evgeny Onegin* as the first work in this genre.[2] Lermontov's *A Hero of Our Time* is obviously another work in the same genre. In this connection, it is worth recalling that Turgenev, in a letter to Katkov, described Bazarov as "really a hero of our time" (4, 303).

The ties of *Fathers and Sons* to *Evgeny Onegin* are not only generic: they extend to matters of composition, style, and thematics. The central quartet of heroes and heroines in Turgenev's novel (Arkady, Bazarov, Katya, and Odintsova) is a variation on a Pushkinian theme. Bazarov's relations to Arkady recalls Onegin's to Lensky. (Note, by the way, that both heroes bear the name Evgeny.) Bazarov, like the coldly rational Onegin, treats his seemingly weak, sentimental friends with condescension and mocks their poetic nature. When Arkady makes a rather florid remark about a falling leaf's resemblance to a butterfly in flight, noting the striking juxtaposition of images of melancholy and joy, death and life, Bazarov cuts him off: "Oh, my friend Arkady Nikolaich—one thing I ask of you: don't talk prettily" (326). Unlike Onegin, Bazarov does not kill his friend, but it is likely that the arrival of Bazarov's father in Chapter XXI prevents a genuine brawl between the two erstwhile friends. Bazarov's rather nasty farewell to Arkady (380-381) reinforces the parallel with *Evgeny Onegin*: two young men who at first seemed good friends separate forever in an atmosphere of muddled recriminations. Finally, like Onegin, Bazarov learns too late that the world is full of surprises—many of them unpleasant. Bazarov, on his death bed, says, "Yes, just try to negate death. It negates you, and that's that!" (391). His words obliquely echo Evgeny Onegin's fate: he had rejected Tatyana—only to find himself rejected by her at the close of Pushkin's novel in verse.

The figures of Odintsova and Katya, by virtue of the structural roles that they play, call to mind Tatyana and Olga. In both cases we are dealing with sisters who live on a country estate and who are courted by "gentlemen callers," one of whom excites particular interest by virtue of the enigma he poses. In addition, Odintsova recalls Tatyana in her independence of thought, her indifference to convention, and her quality of being "different." Moreover, Katya is contrasted to Odintsova in the same was as Olga is to Tatyana: the younger sisters are ordinary young ladies, committed to the norms of their respective societies. All the heroines' attitudes toward their respective heroes are similar. Tatyana and Odintsova are terrified of and fascinated by Onegin and Bazarov, respectively, while Olga's and Katya's attachment to their swains is thoroughly conventional and devoid of passion in the Turgenevian sense of the word.

Fathers and Sons includes scenic allusions to *Evgeny Onegin*. As we recall, Onegin is amazed and appalled by Lensky's interest in Olga:

> "Tell me: which one is Tatyana?"
> "Why, the one who sad
> And silent like Svetlana
> Came in and sat by the window."
> "And you're really in love with the younger one?"
> "And what of it?" "I'd take the other,
> Were I a poet like you.
> There's no life in Olga's features.
> She looks just like the Sistine Madonna:
> Her face is round and red
> Like the stupid moon
> On that stupid horizon."
> Vladimir answered drily
> And afterward was silent all the way home.[3]

There is an inverted mirror image of this situation in *Fathers and Sons*. As Arkady is enthusing over Odintsova, with whom he imagines himself to be in love, Bazarov interrupts him:

> "But it's the sister that's the miracle, not her. . . . She's fresh, untouched, bashful, taciturn, and anything you can mention. She's the one you could get interested in. You could make her into anything you wanted; but the other one—she knows her way around too well."
> Arkady didn't answer Bazarov, and each went to bed with special thoughts in his head. (282)

The point here is not that any parallels between Katya and Tatyana are suggested: rather, the motif of a wordly-wise older friend's pointing out that his naive young comrade is attracted to the wrong sister recalls a similar scene in *Evgeny Onegin*.

Batyuto has pointed out that the duel in *Fathers and Sons* owes much to the similar serio-comic duels in Pushkin's *Evgeny Onegin* and *The Captain's Daughter*.[4] He notes that in all cases the seriousness of the duel is undercut by humorous details, in particular by the presence of a second who is hardly fit for his assignment: Onegin has his Filio, Grinev his Ivan Ignatievich, and Bazarov his Peter (who is, properly speaking, not a second, but a witless witness). An additional kinship between the duels in *Fathers and Sons* and *Evgeny Onegin*—one unremarked by Batyuto—is the fact that both duels are fought over a woman's honor, but in both cases only one of the protagonists is deeply attached to the woman in question. Bazarov's flirtation with Fenechka is not qualitatively different from Onegin's dalliance with Olga. (This is not to imply that Fenechka and Olga have similar personalities. They do not, but the roles that they play in motivating the duels are analogous.) Furthermore, both Onegin and Bazarov realize that the duel they are about to fight is absurd. Onegin thinks to himself:

> He could have shown his feelings,
> And not snarl like a wild animal;
> He ought to have disarmed
> The young heart. "But now
> It's too late; time has flown...
> In addition," he thinks, "the
> Old duelist has butted into this affair;
> He's vicious, a gossip, and wordy...
> Of course one should have contempt
> For his entertaining words,
> But whispers, the laughter of fools..."
> There's social opinion for you!
> The spring of honor, our idol!
> That's what makes the world go round![5]

In short, Onegin agrees to the duel out of vanity. It is also foolish pride that brings Bazarov to the barrier: "It was impossible to refuse; after all, he probably would have struck mè, and then... (Bazarov turned pale at the thought alone; all his pride rose up [in him].)" (349).

Bazarov's behavior at the duel, his refusal to treat it with due seriousness—witness his bantering tone and jokes—evokes the duel in Pushkin's "The Shot," wherein the Count demonstrates similar flippancy by eating cherries from his hat while Silvio takes aim at him.

The Pushkinian themes that Turgenev draws on in *Fathers and Sons* include fate and revolution. It is significant, for instance, that Nikolay reads "The Gypsies," the major theme of which is man's inability to evade his fate: "And everywhere are fatal passions,/And from the Fates there is no defense." Fate is likewise a major theme in *Fathers and Sons,* although Turgenev does not treat it as an exclusively malevolent force. In *Fathers and Sons* the destiny of the sons is to become like their fathers. The irresistible attraction of the fathers' world is emphasized in the novel when Arkady and Bazarov end their wanderings by each returning to his own family estate. (Arkady and Bazarov are prodigal sons, in a sense.) That their homecoming implies a philosophical return to the world of the fathers—even for Bazarov—is suggested when Bazarov drops in at Nikolskoe to tell Arkady about the duel: "Well, so I've headed off for my father's . . . and on the way I dropped in here..." (370). In his description of the duel Bazarov as much as admits that the world of the fathers is one which co-opts a person willy-nilly. That Bazarov is about to join it is implied in the Russian text by the use of the plural of "father": "I have headed off for 'the fathers' [*ja otpravilsia k 'ottsam'*]," i.e., the world of the fathers. Bazarov's capitulation to fate is painful testimony of his personal conviction that life is senseless. Arkady's recognition and acceptance of his fate, by contrast, are relatively painless and ultimately life-affirming. Fate in *Fathers and Sons* seems to be benevolent to the meek, while it strikes down the headstrong and rebellious.

As noted before, the theme of the rebel is a second thematic link between *Fathers and Sons* and Pushkin. In an earlier chapter it was mentioned that as he was creating the figure of Bazarov, Turgenev "dreamed of some sort of strange *pendant* with Pugachev."[6] Batyuto raises the question whether Turgenev had in mind the historical Pugachev or Pushkin's portrait of him in *The Captain's Daughter*, and concludes, reasonably enough, that he had both in view.[7] Similarities shared by Pushkin's Pugachev and Bazarov that Batyuto notes include personalities that unite cruelty and humaneness, and speech patterns that bristle with proverbs and folk sayings. Batyuto goes on to suggest that Grinev's "God forbid we should see a Russian revolt, senseless and merciless" was a sentiment shared by Pushkin himself, and that Turgenev's *Fathers and Sons* as a whole demonstrates Turgenev's Pushkin-like doubts about the desirability of revolution. It should be pointed out, however, that although the theme of the revolutionary does of course link *The Captain's Daughter* with *Fathers and Sons*, Turgenev's reservations about the advisability of revolution are part of the novel's subtext rather than an explicit statement, as in Pushkin's case. On the other hand, Nikolay's socially "progressive" marriage and the fact that at the conclusion of the novel Arkady's management of the estate improves upon his father's are indications of Turgenev's implicit preference for gradual reform over revolution. (Similarly, the positive hero in *Virgin Soil*, Solomin, is a practical man with great common sense, and Turgenev seems to sanction him as Russia's non-heroic hope for a better future.[8]) More importantly, and something that Batyuto either fails or does not allow himself to notice, is that while Pushkin attacks the idea of revolution, Turgenev examines the ideas of a revolutionary, showing them to be naive, insubstantial, and divorced from real life. In the figure of Bazarov he suggests that the revolutionary's motives are in fact anti-democratic and non-humanitarian. Although he draws on the Pushkinian theme of the revolutionary, Turgenev prefigures Dostoevsky's treatment of the revolutionary as a crypto-hater of humanity.

Fathers and Sons likewise draws on several obviously Lermontovian themes and devices. It was observed earlier that Onegin, Pechorin, and Bazarov are all heroes of their time. Another link between Lermontov and *Fathers and Sons* is the role of fate, a theme that plays a large though frustratingly ambiguous role in *A Hero of Our Time*. In respect to thematics, Lermontov is really a disciple of Pushkin so that many of the themes of *Fathers and Sons* are ultimately Pushkinian, with Lermontov serving as a conduit. However, many of the literary devices that Turgenev uses in *Fathers and Sons* are distinctly Lermontovian.

An important instance of a Lermontovian device is the use of a parodic double. Grushnitsky's presence in *A Hero of Our Time* enhances Pechorin's stature, and the same may be said of Sitnikov's role vis-à-vis Bazarov or Kukshina's vis-a-vis Odintsova. Sitnikov provides an eloquent illustration of the distinction between a pseudo-nihilist and a genuine one. Interestingly enough, it was Pisarev who first pointed out similarities between Grushnitsky and Sitnikov,[9] a fact which, along with Pisarev's identification of Bazarov and Pavel as a single personality type, makes one question Reeve's notion that Pisarev's articles on *Fathers and Sons* are not, strictly speaking, literary criticism.[10]

The Lermontovian device of the overheard conversation is also prominent in *Fathers and Sons*. Arkady worries about whether Bazarov has heard his expansive remarks about nature (203); Nikolay overhears Bazarov and Arkady writing off the older generation (238); Bazarov overhears his father (321); Pavel witnesses Bazarov's flirtation with Fenechka (345); Arkady and Katya are unintentionally privy to Bazarov and Odintsova's remarks about them (376); and Bazarov asks the German doctor and his father not to speak Latin in his presence, because he understands it (394). The total number of overheard conversations here does not come close to the thirteen such examples in *A Hero of Our Time* (by Nabokov's count[11]), nor does Turgenev use the device in exactly the same way as Lermontov. In *A Hero of Our Time* overheard conversations are an essential ingredient of the plot—they trigger the narrative action, and without them very little would happen in the novel. In *Fathers and Sons* the device tends to illuminate character or stimulate its revelation: rarely does it speed the plot along or create tension (the exception here is Pavel's overhearing Bazarov and Fenechka in the garden). Nonetheless, Turgenev's frequent reliance on the device summons up the shade of Lermontov.

The process by which the reader uncovers the workings of Bazarov's mind is a subtle variation of the method used by Lermontov in *A Hero of Our Time*. As many Lermontov scholars have pointed out, the novellas in *A Hero of Our Time* are so ordered as to allow us to come gradually closer to Pechorin's mind as intervening narrators are discarded. Thus, in "Bela" we observe Pechorin through the eyes of Maxim Maximych, who is able to reveal precious little about Pechorin's thought processes. In "Maxim Maximych" we see Pechorin from the point of view of the rather more sophisticated anonymous narrator; while the remaining stories, narrated from the first person, confront us directly with Pechorin's thoughts and motivations, such as they are. A similar process can be seen in Turgenev's characterization of Bazarov. Until his stay at Nikolskoe, we see Bazarov largely from other people's perspectives. Characters make remarks about him or we are told directly what they think of him: an instructive example of this is the opening of Chapter X, a virtual catalogue of the attitudes of people at Marino toward Bazarov. Bazarov himself is silent for the most part, and the narrator refrains from any incursions into his mind. Bazarov's uncharacteristic behavior in Odintsova's hotel room (Ch. XV) is noticed by Arkady, but the narrator offers no explanation for the change in Bazarov. Beginning with Bazarov's stay at Nikolskoe, however, the narrator provides substantial third-person analyses of what is taking place in Bazarov's psyche: note, for instance, the long description in Chapter XVIII of Bazarov's confused feelings about Odintsova. In the chapters following his confrontation with the serene landowner, Bazarov himself begins to reveal his state of mind: his remarks to Arkady on the road to his parents' house (306-307) and the exchange between the two friends in the haystack (322-325) are the bext examples of this. On his deathbed Bazarov offers a tortured confession about his past, present, and suddenly foreshortened future. In this pattern of narration which progressively moves away from other characters' observations toward the hero's own thoughts, Turgenev relies heavily on Lermontov's pioneering use of essentially the same device.

One does not normally associate Turgenev with Gogolian traditions, yet there is a Gogolian underside to *Fathers and Sons.* As Fridlender and Batyuto indicate, the town and its inhabitants (Ch. XII-XIV) exude the atmosphere of Gogol's *Dead Souls* and *Inspector General,* above all in regard to the satirical portrayal of provincial bureaucrats.[12] One thinks especially of the President of the Finance Department, who adores summer, when "Each little bee takes its little bribe from each little flower" (255). Matvey Ilich's delight in unmanning his subordinates (254-255) recalls the atrophied personality of the Very Important Person in Gogol's "The Overcoat." Even the names of people in town—Kolyazin, Sitnikov, Evdoksiya Nikitishna Kukshina—have a vaguely Gogolian ring. The strongest link between Turgenev and Gogol is the use of caricature—a device that Turgenev rejected in principle (just as he rejected but occasionally used Tolstoyan repetition).[13] The combination of caricature and setting—a dismal provincial backwater—allies Turgenev with the Gogol tradition.

Batyuto suggests that the portrait of Bazarov's parents is also Gogolian: he particularly has in mind here Gogol's "Old World Landowners."[14] He traces parallels between Bazarov's mother and Pulkheria Ivanovna, both of whom are superstitious and whose lives seem to center around thoughts about food, its preparation and its consumption. But there is also a link with *Evgeny Onegin* here, especially if we compare the pre-history of Tatyana's mother with that of Bazarov's mother. Both are pretentiously educated gentry women who, because of life in the country, abandon the airs of their youth and become countrified and Russified. Pushkin's narrator tells us of Tatyana's mother:

> She used to write with blood
> In the albums of tender maidens,

> Called Praskovia Polina,
> And spoke singingly,
> Wore a very tight corset,
> And knew how to pronounce
> A Russian N nasally, as in French;
> But soon all this gave way:
> The corset, the album, Princess Aline,
> The notebook of sentimental verse
> She forgot them [all]; Began to call
> The former Celine Akulka,
> And finally renovated her
> Quilted cap and dressing gown.[15]

We find some of the same motifs in the pre-history of Bazarov's mother:

> In her youth she had been quite comely, played the clavichord and chattered a little French; but in the course of many years' wanderings with her husband, whom she married against her will, she grew stout and forgot her music and French. (317)

A more convincing argument for Gogolian influence in the portrait of Bazarov's parents is the description of their house, a description which is quite Gogolian in its use of a lengthy, chaotic catalogue of objects to characterize the home's inhabitants:

> His [Bazarov's father's] home consisted of six tiny rooms. One of them—the room into which he led our friends—was called the study. A fat-legged table, heaped up with papers that had turned black with anient dust and looked as if they had been smoked, occupied the entire space between the two windows; on the walls hung Turkish rifles, whips, a saber, two maps, some anatomical drawings, a portrait of Hufeland, a monogram woven from hair set in a black frame, and a diploma under glass; a leather sofa, ripped and ragged in places, stood between two huge cupboards of Karelian birch; on the shelves were crowded together in disorder books, little boxes, stuffed birds, jars, phials; in a corner stood a broken electrical apparatus. (310)

The use of objects to characterize their owner is not specifically Gogolian by any means, but this sort of cataloguing—both in its extensiveness and its bizarreness—speaks for Gogol's influence.

Thus, we see that in *Fathers and Sons* Turgenev continues the traditions of all his major Russian predecessors. The heritage of

Pushkin's and Lermontov's Romantic heroes reveals itself in the *raznochinets* Bazarov, and the town and Bazarov's parents remind us that Gogol is more important for Turgenev than we might at first assume.

Fathers and Sons indicates, in addition, directions that the Russian novel was to take, both in the immediate era of the 1860s and in some cases on down to the present day. We have already noted, for instance, that *Fathers and Sons* has its generic roots in the "culture-heroed" works of Pushkin and Lermontov. But even though Bazarov is the central hero of the novel he is surrounded by a cast of diverse characters through whom Turgenev depicts not only the hero of his time, but the milieu as well. In this way *Fathers and Sons* prefigures a general trend in the evolution of the Russian novel. Milton Ehre writes:

> With the sixties Russian novelists began to concentrate their energies upon depicting the intricate fabric of social life; Turgenev, whose novels first appeared toward the end of the previous decade, anticipated the trend. As a result, the Russian novel became decentralized, shifting from a single dominant protagonist to a wide spectrum of characters representative of different social groups . . . . The more explicit social concerns of the novel were complemented by an increased dramatic emphasis, often expressive of social conflict.[16]

And as Gippius points out, it is specifically with *Fathers and Sons* that the center of gravity in Turgenev's novels begins to shift from the hero to the milieu.[17]

Fathers and Sons, however, is not simply a novel of social conflict. It is also a novel about ideas. We say this, knowing full well that Turgenev was always much more interested in personalities than ideas. But, as Matlaw observes, the characters in *Fathers and Sons* and the ideas they represent are inseparable.[18] For this reason we have every right to consider Turgenev's novel an ideological novel. Here *Fathers and Sons* once again prefigures a major trend, for it is not simply an ideological novel: it is the *first* Russian ideological novel. Specifically, it is the first anti-nihilist novel in Russian literature, and as such it spawned hosts of pro-nihilist and anti-nihilist works of fiction. Charles Moser has written extensively on the subject, and it is indicative that we find already in *Fathers and Sons* examples of all the major types of nihilists that Moser isolates in anti-nihilist fiction. Moser's three main types include: (1) young radicals who keep their faith even though some of their colleagues do not, (2) honest young people temporarily led astray by radicalism, and (3) frauds and criminals.[19] Bazarov is an example of the first type, Arkady of the second, and Sitnikov and Kukshina of the third.

Furthermore, *Fathers and Sons* is the first link in a polemical series of important symptomatic ideological works of the 1860s and 1870s. Chernyshevsky's *What Is to Be Done?*, one of whose heroes bears the name Kirsanov, and Sleptsov's *Hard Times (Trudnoe vremia)*, whose nihilist hero Riazanov recruits disciples, are both polemical reactions to *Fathers and Sons*.[20] All the major and numerous minor writers of the era reacted to Chernyshevky's and Sleptsov's works with anti-nihilist novels. Among the works we might mention are Pisemsky's *Troubled Seas (Vzbalamuchennoe more)*, Leskov's *No Way Out (Nekuda)* and *At Dagger's Drawn (Na nozhakh)*, and Goncharov's *The Abyss (Obryv)*.[21] Even Tolstoy's *War and Peace*, it will be recalled, began as an anti-nihilist work.[22] By far the most significant anti-nihilist novels are Dostoevsky's *Notes from Underground* (itself in part a parody of *What Is to be Done?*[23]), *Crime and Punishment,* and *The Possessed.*

Turgenev maintained that Dostoevsky was one of the only two people who completely understood his intentions in *Fathers and Sons*.[24] We do not know exactly what it is that Dostoevsky wrote to Turgenev, because his letter is not extant. We do have Turgenev's reply to it, however, and it indicates that Dostoevsky had reacted to *Fathers and Sons* with praise and what Turgenev saw as insight (4, 358-359). That should not surprise us, because in Bazarov one perceives an embryonic Dostoevsky hero, and Turgenev's novel as a whole prefigures many themes and methods used by Dostoevsky in his mature novels.

Fathers and Sons and Dostoevsky's novels represent a very special sort of ideological novel. They are not simply novels of ideas. Bakhtin's comments on Engelgardt are pertinent in this connection:

> B. M. Engelgardt proceeds from the sociological and cultural-historical definition of Dostoevsky's hero, Dostoevsky's hero is the *raznochinets* intellectual cut off from the cultural tradition, the soil and the land— the representative of an "accidental tribe." Such a man enters into a special relationship with the idea: he is defenseless before it and its power, for he is not firmly rooted in life and is deprived of any cultur-

al tradition. He becomes the "man of an idea," a man possessed by an idea. The idea becomes in him an "idea-force," which omnipotently defines and distorts his consciousness and his life. The idea leads an independent life in the hero's consciousness: it is in fact not he who lives but the idea, and the novelist describes not the hero's life, but the life of an idea in him; the historian of the "accidental tribe" becomes the "historiographer of an idea." Therefore, in place of the biographical dominant of the usual type (as in Tolstoy or Turgenev, for example), the dominant of the hero's representation is the idea which possessed him. Hence originates the definition of Dostoevsky's novel as an "ideological novel."[25]

Engelgardt speaks specifically of Dostoevsky's novels—note that he contrasts them with Turgenev's—but what he says is as accurate a description of Turgenev's *Fathers and Sons* as it is of Dostoevsky's works. Byaly points out that it was Strakhov who first suggested that one of Bazarov's perculiarities was that he was "a man of theory, and a theory created him," and that Strakhov observed this decades before Engelgardt wrote on the ideological novel.[26]

Bakhtin argues that the role of the idea in Dostoevsky's novels is unique, because it merges with personality, becoming inseparable from it. In Bakhtin's words:

> The hero in Dostoevsky is not only a word about himself and about his immediate environment, but also a word about the world: he has not only a consciousness, but an ideology, too. . . . The truth about the world, according to Dostoevsky, is inseparable from the truth of the personality. The categories of self-consciousness which determined life already in the case of Devushkin, and especially in the case of Golyadkin, —acceptance or non-acceptance, revolt or meekness—in the novels become the basic categories of thought about the world. Therefore the loftier principles of *Weltanschauung* are the same as the principles of the most concrete personal experience. Thus is achieved the artistic merging of personal life with *Weltanschauung*, of intimate experience with the idea, which is so characteristic of Dostoevsky.[28]

But all of this is equally true of the idea and personality in *Fathers and Sons*. To draw on Matlaw again,

> [In *Fathers and Sons*] Turgenev has fused the character and his political or social view. . . . Pavel Kirsanov's or any other character's views in *Fathers and Sons, are* that person, and present not a statement or an argument about a topical question, but rather use that statement to

characterize the person uttering it.[28]

There is of course a qualitative difference between the ideas at work in Bazarov and those which literally consume Kirillov or Ivan Karamazov, for instance. Nonetheless it would be foolish to deny a genetic and generic link between Turgenev's ideological novel and Dostoevsky's.

It was stated earlier that Bazarov is a proto-Dostoevskian hero: a comparison of *Fathers and Sons* with *Crime and Punishment* and *The Possessed* reveals analogies that are instructive. Raskolnikov resembles Bazarov in a number of ways. Like Bazarov, he is a young radical who has come from the provinces to St. Petersburg to study. As Byaly points out, Dostoevsky's characterization of Raskolnikov as "sullen, glum, haughty, and proud" might describe Bazarov just as well.[29] Both heroes have strained relations with their adoring families, and both seem equally capable of good and evil. As Byaly also remarks, both heroes are tragically divided against themselves: their hearts and minds are at war.[30] Bazarov asserts that there is no mystery involved in relations between men and women (226). His theory collapses when put to the test at Nikolskoe. Bazarov's ideas, potent as they may be, are shown to be alienated from the norms of human experience (as Turgenev perceives and portrays them). Dostoevsky's treatment of Raskolnikov, as Byaly suggests, is fundamentally the same: Raskolnikov puts his various conflicting theories to the test in the pawnbroker's flat and in doing so proves them all wrong, at least insofar as they apply to him. Both Bazarov and Raskolnikov claim to be super-human, and both learn that they are not. In Freeborn's opinion, "Bazarov is close to Dostoevsky's man-God in his arrogance and self-will."[31] Thus Dostoevsky adopts a strategy first used by Turgenev in *Fathers and Sons*: rather than directly and authorially attacking the hero's notions, he permits the hero himself to discover the tragic inadequacy of his theories. This is a technique Dostoevsky uses in all his ideological novels, and it is prefigured in *Fathers and Sons.*

There are similarities not only between Bazarov and Raskolnikov, but between Arkady and Razumikhin as well. Both are average, common-sensical young men who instinctively know more about life than do their ostensibly more intelligent friends. At the conclusion of *Crime and Punishment* we become aware that Raskolnikov has no answers to the questions he poses, and that his knowledge of the world and himself is virtually nil. We also realize that Razumikhin has all the correct answers (partly, of course, because he does not ask any of the "accursed questions"): he has sensed all along that Raskolnikov is the murderer and that he is nonetheless a decent fellow. Razumikhin's marriage to Dunya, their love for each other and their unextravagant plans for the future suggest precisely the sort of alternative that the limited, but happy Kirsanov and Katya incarnate in *Fathers and Sons*.

As an additional link between Razumikhin and *Fathers and Sons*, Byaly argues that Razumikhin's ironical comment, "And thus it follows that if one organizes society correctly, all crime will cease immediately," is practically a direct citation of Bazarov's "Correct society, and there will be no [moral] illnesses" (277).[32] It may be just that, although it seems equally likely that Dostoevsky was quoting Chernyshevsky.

The importance of *Fathers and Sons* for *The Possessed* is even greater than for *Crime and Punishment*. Turgenev in general had a great deal to do with Dostoevsky's novel, which had not yet even been published in its entirety when readers began speculating on the nature and extent of Turgenev's role as unbidden muse for Dostoevsky.[33] It was obvious to all that the figure of Karmazinov, "the great writer," was a caricature of Turgenev. As early as April 24/ May 6, 1871, we find Turgenev writing to Yakov Polonsky: "They've been telling me that Dostoevsky has caricatured me. Well, so what! Let him have his fun" (9, 85). Moreover, Turgenev apparently realized that Dostoevsky's irate imagination had been inflamed by *Smoke* (1867). In the same letter to Polonsky, Turgenev goes on to say: "He [Dostoevsky] came to see me about five years ago in Baden—not to pay me back the money he had borrowed from me—but to swear at me for all he was worth for *Smoke*, which, in his opinion, should have been burned at the hand of the executioner." At approximately the same time that Turgenev was writing to Polonsky, Apollon Maykov was telling Dostoevsky that the characters in *The Possessed* seemed to be "Turgenev's heroes in their old age."[34] Thus, Turgenev and Dostoevsky's own contemporaries were already aware that both Turgenev *and* his works figure in Dostoevsky's polemical novel.

Twentieth-century scholarship has expanded our understanding of the links between Turgenev and *The Possessed*. Focusing on the portrait of Karmazinov, A. S. Dolinin, Yu. Nikolsky, and I. S. Zilberstein have elucidated the manifold reasons underlying Dostoevsky's nearly rabid distaste for Turgenev and his later works.³⁵ M. S. Altman has suggested, and rightly so, that Turgenev, as a leading representative of the generation of the 1840s, is one of the prototypes for Stepan Verkhovensky as well as for Karmazinov.³⁶ Scholars so far have identified at least ten of Turgenev's works that are reflected in the text of *The Possessed.*³⁷

The two Turgenev works that most contributed to the genesis of *The Possessed* were *Smoke* and *Fathers and Sons.* There is a curious development to be noted in this regard. As Soviet scholars have shown, it was *Smoke* that provided one of the major impulses for Dostoevsky to write *The Possessed.*³⁸ Enraged by Turgenev's Westernizing exposé of Russia's cultural, philosophical, and political shallowness, Dostoevsky was moved to launch a defensive counterattack. And for the polemical response to *Smoke* Dostoevsky drew on materials from *Fathers and Sons.* (It is one of the greater ironies of Russian literary history, by the way, that in his attempt to dispel the gloom and darkness of *Smoke,* Dostoevsky produced a novel whose bleakness far surpasses even Turgenev's pessimistic portrait of Russia.)

That Dostoevsky had *Fathers and Sons* at the back of his mind as he began work on *The Possessed* is beyond question. Using Dostoevsky's notebooks, for instance, N. F. Budanova has shown that the original outlines for *The Possessed* look very much like Turgenev's novel. ³⁹ Moreover, she argues that Peter Verkhovensky is a debased Bazarov.⁴⁰ Illuminating and well-documented as the accumulated findings of Budanova and other scholars are, however, they do not tell the whole story.

In *The Possessed* Dostoevsky conducts a complex, multi-levelled polemic with Turgenev the man and the writer, as well as with his most controversial hero, Bazarov. Dostoevsky deals with Turgenev and Bazarov similarly, refracting their personalities, views, and biographies into a number of contrasting facets which he then redistributes among his own characters and for his own purposes. Dostoevsky rings at least three variations on Bazarov: (1) the unlikeable, strident, and potentially dangerous nihilist, (2) the sullen, haughty, and enigmatic Romantic, and (3) the noble, but deeply flawed tragic hero for whom death triggers redemptive self-knowledge. When subjected to Dostoevsky's imaginative and malicious dissection, Turgenev himself emerges in two guises: (1) the immensely vain, pretentious, and left-leaning "great writer," and (2) the "distinguished" but somewhat seedy elder spokesman for the generation of the 1840s whose credibility is compromised by his slavish attachment to a domineering woman and his status as an absentee father. Elements from Turgenev and Bazarov occasionally are melded into a single character, e.g., Stepan Verkhovensky.

Let us begin a more detailed analysis with Bazarov *qua* nihilist. As Budanova notes, both in an article, and in the commentary to Volume XII of the Academy edition now in progress,[41] Dostoevsky's February 1870 sketches for the novel reveal thematic and compositional parallels with *Fathers and Sons*. A "nihilist" arrives at a gentry estate, argues with local aristocrats, makes a trip to the provincial capital, and has a romance with a society woman (XII, 173). Furthermore, this "nihilist," the embryonic Peter Verkhovensky, frequently is designated as Bazarov in Dostoevsky's notes.[42] Budanova concludes that Peter Verkhovensky is "a sort of lowered and banalized Bazarov, lacking his intellect and 'great heart,'[43] but at the same time with incredibly inflated 'Bazarovism' " (XII, 175).

Budanova's conclusion is accurate, even though in her argumentation she overlooks a number of additional motifs linking Bazarov and Peter Verkhovensky. Consider, for instance, Peter's conversation with Stavrogin on the way to the secret meeting:

> "Why, the central committee is you and me, and there will be as many branches as you wish."
> "But what human filth!"
> "They're material. Even they will do." (X, 299)

That dialogue is a direct allusion to the question that Arkady puts to Bazarov about Sitnikov:

> "Why on earth did that stupid Sitnikov have to drop in?"
> Bazarov at first stirred in his bed, and then said the following:
> "My friend, I see that you are still stupid. Sitnikovs are essential to us. I—make sure you understand this—I need such fools. After all, it's not for gods to glaze pottery!..." (VIII, 346)

The point here, of course, is that Bazarov and Peter share a worldview grounded in arrogance and contempt for mankind.

Bazarov and Peter both see themselves as educators for the older generation. Bazarov observes Nikolay Kirsanov reading Pushkin and tells Arkady to give his father something more worthwhile, say, Büchner's *Stoff and Kraft*. In *The Possessed*, Peter discovers Chernyshevsky's *What Is to Be Done?* on his father's table: " 'So you're enlightening yourself?" Peter Stepanovich smirked, after taking the book from the table and reading the title. 'It's high time. I'll bring you some even better stuff, if you want' " (X, 238). The fathers' responses to their reading materials present a sharp contrast. Pavel Kirsanov simply fails to make any sense out of Büchner at all (240), but Stepan Verkhovensky ruefully admits that Chernyshevsky's ideas are essentially those of his own generation's (X, 238). This, as a matter of fact, is the central thesis in *The Possessed*: the men of the 1840s are responsible for the extremism of the young men of the 1860s.

The link between Bazarov and Peter Verkhovensky is further underlined in one of Stepan Verkhovensky's frequent tirades:

> *"Passons,"* he started up again five minutes later. "I really don't understand Turgenev. That Bazarov of his is such a contrived character that he couldn't possibly exist. They themselves were the first to repudiate him, declaring that he was like nothing on earth. Bazarov is some sort of murky mixture of Gogol's Nozdrev and Byron, *c'est le mot.* Just take a look at them: they turn somersaults and squeal with joy like puppies in the sun; they're happy; they're the conquerors. Byron indeed! They're simply dull! They've the irritable vanity of cooks, a vulgar longing *de faire du bruit autour de son nom,* without realizing what *son nom*... Ah, what a caricature he is! I tell him, 'Do you really, by any chance, wish to offer yourself as a substitute for Christ, just the way you are?' *Il rit. Il rit beaucoup, il rit trop.* He has a strange kind of smile. I don't understand—his mother didn't have a smile like that. *Il rit toujours.*" (X, 171)

What is important to note here is that although Stepan begins talking about Bazarov, he concludes with remarks about his son, so that in fact in the central portion of his peroration he may be referring either to Bazarov or to Peter or to both. In other words, Bazarov and Peter are identified in Stepan's imagination, as they are in Dostoevsky's.

For one of the more amusing parallels between Bazarov and the younger Verkhovensky, we recall the circumstances surrounding Pavel Kirsanov's challenge to Bazarov. Pavel comes to Bazarov's room, bringing with him his elegant walking stick *(trost)*, which he rarely uses (346). The menace lurking in the stick is not lost on Bazarov. Significantly, we learn in *The Possessed* that at one point Stepan Verkhovensky has chased his son out of the house with a stick *(palka)*, after an argument that *he had initiated himself* (X, 237). Here it is worth recalling the February sketches, where the relationship between Granovsky (as Stepan is identified there) and "the student," Bazarov, is characterized by the latter's indifferent replies, Granovsky's eagerness to embroil him in debate, and the student's sudden flare-up (XI, 72). All of this resembles Pavel Kirsanov and Bazarov's behavior at mealtimes (218-221, 241-149). Hence, it is most appropriate that the stick with which Pavel Kirsanov might have struck Bazarov resurfaces in the hands of Stepan Verkhovensky, who apparently does lay into his son with it.

The relations between Pavel Kirsanov and Bazarov, on the one hand, and Stepan Verkhovensky and his son Peter, on the other, serve to emphasize the fundamental similarities between the generations rather than their differences. As we observed earlier, in Chapter III of this monograph, Pavel and Bazarov are ideological antipodes, but similar personality types. In an analogous way, Stepan Verkhovensky and Peter seem to be at daggers drawn, yet they exhibit common traits. Both are egoistical rhetoricians, not to say windbags, and both are "very dangerous," to quote Herzen.[44] Peter is directly responsible for the whirlwind of destruction that erupts at the novel's conclusion, while his father is indirectly, but deeply culpable, since he was Stavrogin's tutor. Through the latter he has sown the seeds of moral and political chaos. Thus, to return to the discussion of the stick that passes from Pavel Kirsanov's hands into Stepan Verkhovensky's, it is but a symbol of the notion that the high-minded principles of the men of the 1840s are only skin deep, that just beneath them is concealed the specter of violence—a trait that the younger generation inherits.

By now it should be obvious that Budanova's observations about the relationship between Bazarov and Peter Verkhovensky are well-founded. They should be amended, however, for it is not Bazarov *in toto* who is caricatured in the younger Verkhovensky, but only one aspect of Turgenev's hero—his "Bazarovism," i.e., his militant and arrogant maximalism. Indeed, for all the similarities between Bazarov and Peter, the differences between the two are glaring. Peter is a chatterbox, a sort of prattling *perpetuum mobile,* while Bazarov is characterized largely by an enigmatic taciturnity. It is precisely this latter quality that accounts for Dostoevsky's second vision of Bazarov—Bazarov the Romantic hero.

The characterization of Stavrogin employs a technique similar to the one that Turgenev uses for Bazarov. Surrounded by a haze of mystery, Stavrogin rarely deigns to speak. The narrator takes pains, for instance, to emphasize Stavrogin's unearthly silence during the scandal scene in Mrs. Stavrogina's parlor. If we overlook the problematical confession ("At Tikhon's"), we are almost completely dependent upon other characters' remarks about Stavrogin until the very end of the novel when he reveals something of himself in his note to Dasha (X, 513-515) and even more of himself in his suicide. Although Stavrogin does not figure in Dostoevsky's earliest plans for *The Possessed,* the fact that he nonetheless began work on the novel with thoughts of Bazarov in mind suggests that Stavrogin's quizzical silence, not to mention his Satanic pride and magnetic effect on others, can be traced at least in part to Turgenev's hero.[45]

Stavrogin's ties with Bazarov are further emphasized by the relationship between Stavrogin and Peter Verkhovensky, one that parallels Bazarov's with Sitnikov. Sitnikov fancies himself a progressive young nihilist, but he is really an unprincipled hanger-on who seems to spend most of his time trying to track down Bazarov. Having looked for him at his hotel, Sitnikov finally comes across Bazarov on the street, although Bazarov keeps right on walking as Sitnikov runs after him and Arkady (256-257). Later in the novel Sitnikov shows up at Odintsova's estate just as Bazarov and Arkady are about to leave (VIII, 301). Furthermore, it is Sitnikov who introduces Bazarov and Arkady to the local proponent of "progressive ideas," Kukshina. The portrait of Peter Verkhovensky would seem to owe something to Sitnikov's. Peter too is an unprincipled fraud who spends a great deal of his time looking for Stavrogin. The scene of the prattling Sitnikov chasing down the street after Bazarov is refracted in *The Possessed* when Stavrogin refuses to make room for Peter on the sidewalk, thus forcing him to walk in the mud (X, 298). It is Peter who introduces Stavrogin to the local revolutionary circle. Moreover, Sitnikov and Peter snigger and giggle almost as much as they chatter on the run.[46] Here it should be noted that because Dostoevsky adapts various facets of Bazarov's personality instead of Bazarov as a totality, the Stavrogin-Peter Verkhovensky pairing allows Dostoevsky to play off Bazarov the Romantic hero against Bazarov the nihilist.

The final refraction of Bazarov in *The Possessed* is the noble but flawed tragic hero whose death brings belated self-awareness. This aspect of Dostoevsky's polyvision surfaces in the pages devoted to Stepan Verkhovensky's death, a scene that is saturated with details reminiscent of Bazarov's final days and hours. Note, for instance, that as Stepan lies ill and dying, he discovers all manner of unpleasant truths about himself: "My friend, I've lied all my life. Even when I was telling the truth. And I never spoke for the sake of the truth, but only for myself. I knew that even before, but it's only now that I see it" (X, 497). Suddenly a carriage comes rumbling up and out steps Varvara Stavrogina. Odintsova's arrival at Bazarov's deathbed comes to mind immediately. Moreover, Varvara Stavrogina and Odintsova share certain traits: both are widows with good business sense and a frosty curiosity about the world. Stepan Verkhovensky confesses to an unforgiving Varvara that he has loved her: "*Je vous aimais!*" (X, 501). Similarly, Bazarov affirms his past love for Odintsova: "Well, what can I tell you... I loved you!" (395). In order to calm him, Odintsova offers him water (396), a gesture that Varvara Stavrogina repeats for Stepan (X, 501). Bazarov goes on to proclaim the wrongness of his earlier views about himself and his place in the world. Finally, when he is near death, his father begs him to accept the final rites: "Evgeny, you're better now; God grant that you'll recover, but take advantage of this time, console your mother and me, fulfil your Christian duty!" (292). The issue of last rites for an atheist reappears in *The Possessed*, when Varvara tells Stepan:

> "Stepan Trofimovich, one needs to foresee everything. I have sent for a priest. You must fulfil your duty..."
> Knowing his convictions, she was extraordinarily afraid that he would refuse. He looked at her with surprise. (X, 504).

The parallels do not end even here. Just as we are presented with a portrait of Bazarov's grave, so the narrator of *The Possessed* makes a few modest remarks about Stepan Verkhovensky's final resting place (X, 506). The sheer number of overlapping details in these two death scenes does not admit of coincidence.

Dostoevsky's letter to Apollon Maykov provides additional confirmation of the notion that Bazarov's tragic self-redemption in the face of death is objectified in the description of Stepan

Verkhovensky's final days. In response to Maykov's observation that the characters in *The Possessed* seemed to be "Turgenev's heroes in their old age," Dostoevsky wrote: "Brilliant! While writing I myself had something like that in mind, but in three words you have delineated this with a formula."[47] Unless we acknowledge an implied link between Bazarov and Stepan Verkhovensky, Maykov's and Dostoevsky's remarks are incomprehensible. After all, who in the novel *The Possessed* is in his old age if not Stepan? Furthermore, by granting Stepan a belated tragic grandeur, Dostoevsky pays his ambiguous respects to the similarly exalted stature that Bazarov earns through his heroic confrontation with death and himself. The respects *are* ambiguous, however, since even as Stepan acquires a certain tragic aura, he remains a comical and absurd figure. By immersing Bazarov in such a double-edged context, Dostoevsky likewise suggests that Turgenev's hero, for all his magnetism cannot be taken completely seriously. And indeed, Bazarov's actions and remarks are occasionally ludicrous, but how then are we to explain Dostoevsky's documented admiration for *Fathers and Sons* and its hero?

Dostoevsky's non-extant, but apparently enthusiastic letter to Turgenev about *Fathers and Sons* has already been mentioned. And then there is the matter of Dostoevsky's comment in "Winter Notes of Summer Impressions": "Well, and didn't he [Turgenev] get it for Bazarov, the restless and yearning Bazarov (the trait of a great heart), in spite of all his nihilism" (V, 59). If one is to bring Dostoevsky's pronouncements on *Fathers and Sons* to bear on *The Possessed*, however, it would be wise to take into account a number of factors. On the one hand, Dostoevsky's laudatory letter to Turgenev and "Winter Notes on Summer Impressions" date from the early 1860s. Nearly a decade had passed by the time that Dostoevsky began work on *The Possessed*. As we know, Dostoevsky was not incapable of radical shifts in his views. Moreover, he was not beyond dissimulation. His own correspondence testifies to the fact that although he sent Turgenev a letter full of praise for "Phantoms," he told another correspondent that he found the story sickly and senile.[48] Along the same lines, it is worth recalling that Dostoevsky's recorded remarks about Bazarov were made at that time when he was grooming Turgenev as a potential contributor for his journals *Time* and *Epoch*. All of these considerations serve to put so many question marks around Dostoevsky's published or presumed statements about *Fathers and Sons* as to undermine completely their value as critical tools. Dostoevsky's attitude toward Turgenev, *Fathers and Sons,* and Bazarov is best studied through the novel *The Possessed.* We will return to this point.

The question of the elements of Turgenev himself used in *The Possessed* has been generally well-researched. The parodic bases for the portrait of Karmazinov, the "great writer," for instance, would seem to have been studied to exhaustion.[49] Altman opened up a new and fruitful line of investigation when he suggested that Turgenev was a prototype for Stepan Verkhovensky as well as for Karmazinov.[50] He argues that as a leading elder Westernizer, Turgenev is automatically a model for the elder Verkhovensky.[51] Moreover, he notes that Stepan Verkhovensky's situation vis-à-vis Varvara Stavrogina is not unlike Turgenev's lifelong attachment to Pauline Viardot, a relationship in which Turgenev invariably acceded to Viardot's wishes and desires.[52] The parallels can and should be pressed further. It will be recalled, for instance, that Turgenev spent most of his adult life as an appendage to the Viardot household, where his status was similar to Stepan Verkhovensky's at the Stavrogin estate. In addition, up until the arrival of Peter Verkhovensky and Stavrogin in town, Stepan Verkhovensky has seen his son only twice in his life. The child was packed off to distant aunts at a tender age and raised by them. Turgenev initially dealt with Polina, his illegitimate daughter, in no less high-handed a manner. For the first eight years of her life he simply forgot about her. Then, suddenly, in the 1850s, he dispatched her to Western Europe to be raised by Pauline Viardot. It is true that from then on Turgenev was more than good to his daughter, even if he saw her relatively infrequently. The fact remains, however, that Turgenev and Stepan Verkhovensky are absentee fathers.[53]

If these surmises are correct, i.e., that behind Stepan Verkhovensky and Varvara Stavrogina stand the shadows of Turgenev and Mme. Viardot, Stepan's final scenes acquire added richness of literary and extra-literary allusion. Here we are dealing with three pairs of protagonists:

Stepan Verkhovensky — Varvara Stavrogina
Bazarov — Odintsova
Turgenev — Pauline Viardot

That Varvara Stavrogina, Odintsova, and Pauline Viardot are all linked is not really very surprising, since they are three dominant, not to say domineering women of the world who have their male admirers under their thumbs. But what do Stepan Verkhovensky, Bazarov, and Turgenev have in common? For the answer to that question, we turn to the February notes for *The Possessed,* where Dostoevsky remarks:

> Bazarov was written by a man of the '40s and without affectation, and it's obvious that a man of the '40s couldn't have written Bazarov without violating the truth.
> "How is he distorted?"
> "He's put on a pedestal, that's how." (XI, 72)

Thus, for Dostoevsky, the men of the 1840s, i.e., Westernizers, are distorters of the truth, or to use a less elegant formulation, they are liars ("I've lied my whole life," says Stepan Verkhovensky). Therefore, within the system of associations that Dostoevsky has created in *The Possessed,* Turgenev, by virtue of his ties with Stepan, is a proponent of falsehoods, just as his hero Bazarov is the incarnation of foolish self-deception. So, within the final pages of *The Possessed,* Stepan Verkhovensky, Bazarov, and Turgenev merge into a single type: the Westernizer. And for Dostoevsky the Westernizer, regardless of his age or class, is a nihilist. Note, moreover, that the context in which these three figures overlap in Dostoevsky's imagination is one that is both tragic and comic. These two polarities—the tragic and the comic—are parallel emanations from a single source in *The Possessed*—wrongheadedness.

What general conclusions are to be made about the complex relations among Turgenev, Bazarov, and *The Possessed?* Firstly, it should be apparent that any attempt to define Dostoevsky's attitude toward Bazarov is impossible without taking *The Possessed* into account.[54] Secondly, *Fathers and Sons* was an inspiration for *The Possessed* far beyond Dostoevsky's original work on the novel.[55] In a sense *The Possessed* is an extended commentary on *Fathers and Sons.* One might even call it Dostoevsky's "corrected" version of Turgenev's novel. The "corrections" run along two parallel tracks. On the one hand, Dostoevsky portrays Bazarovism, in all its manifestations, i.e., in the characters of Stavrogin and the two Verkhovenskys, as lethal. In *Fathers and Sons* Bazarov quite literally self-destructs. His death is the equivalent of suicide. He ultimately fails to infect the other figures in the novel with his own metaphysical malaise, however. Such optimism is hardly the case in *The Possessed,* where the combined actions of Stavrogin, Stepan Verkhovensky, and Peter Verkhovensky—all of them Bazarovs metamorphosized within Dostoevsky's creative laboratory—result in madness and mayhem that leave few untouched, not to mention alive.

On the other hand, by refracting aspects of Turgenev and his creation, Bazarov, among so many doomed and dangerous figures in *The Possessed,* Dostovesky suggests that the sins of the Westernizing sons are but amplifications of the sins of their fathers. The older generation is responsible, in an exclusively negative way, for the mores of the younger generation. That is not so in *Fathers and Sons,* where Nikolay Kirsanov is presumably to be thanked for his son's positive traits—moderation, his love of nature and art, and his lack of egoism. There is no such optimistic alternative in the bleak house of Russia that Dostoevsky portrays in *The Possessed.* All are guilty there, and most are punished. But the guilty parties are all Westernizers, and this is Dostoevsky's ultimate response to Turgenev's *Smoke.* By refashioning *Fathers and Sons* for his own purposes, Dostoevsky rejects the Westernizing attack on Russia manifested in *Smoke.* Where Turgenev sees Russia's salvation with the West, Dostoevsky sees only her destruction. His positive alternative vision, "the star rising in the East," was to find its expression in *The Brothers Karamazov,* a novel that once again returns to the very Turgenevian theme of fathers and sons.

Just as *Fathers and Sons* prefigures and occasions themes and techniques in Dostoevsky's works, so it touches on certain Tolstoyan concerns. The two most obvious are the apotheosis of domestic life and the study of the effects of time. *War and Peace* is a paean to the family, man's primary obligations to it, and the spiritual satisfaction derived from the fulfillment of those obligations. Turgenev holds out a kind of proto-Tolstoyan vision of domestic happiness in the figures of Arkady, Nikolay, and their wives and children. One aspect of Tolstoy's glorification of the family is his study of the differences between generations, differences which are reconciled by the passage of time. As Matlaw notes:

> Normally the problem of generations is solved by time: the sons gradually move toward their permanent positions, give over being "angry

young men," and become husbands and fathers, angry or not. It is perhaps the hardest subject of all to handle, as the reaction to the end of *War and Peace,* with its assertion of domestic permanence, and in *Fathers and Sons,* the quick taming of Arkady Kirsanov prove: the world of struggle and aspiration is more interesting to contemplate than that of fixity and acceptance.[56]

Turgenev's vision of domestic permanence and his study of the effects of time are only hints of what Tolstoy will do with these themes. As a colleague once noted:

The option of domestic quietude that Turgenev presents is an uneasy, unconvincing "alternative," partly because the ideas of continuity, regeneration, and the ebb and flow of life that Tolstoy works so perfectly into *his* novels are missing in Turgenev, or simply slid in at the end of the novel.[57]

Those elements are not missing: they are present in embryonic form, as the novel's very title suggests. They are, however, very definitely "slid in" quickly at the novel's conclusion. We *see* time's effects in *Fathers and Sons,* just as we do in Tolstoy, but we do not sense their inevitability as we do in Tolstoy. That is no doubt a function of the scale on which Tolstoy works. Moreover, there is another crucial distinction between Turgenev and Tolstoy. Nature and eternity in *Fathers and Sons* are utterly indifferent: they bestow their bounties and reap their harvests with complete arbitrariness. In *War and Peace,* on the other hand, nature and eternity are profoundly beneficent: death is not a tragedy precisely *because* it is a part of the natural cycle.

Turgenev's masterpiece suggests general directions for the Russian novel in the hands of other writers, too, and in still other ways. It is *Fathers and Sons,* for instance, whose very title provides a convenient formulation of the theme that has continued to occupy Russian writers up to the present day. George Steiner speaks of "fathers and sons" as the central theme of the works of Turgenev, Dostoevsky, and Tolstoy.[58] Twentieth-century writers as diverse as Bely (*St. Petersburg*), Olesha (*Envy*), Bulgakov (*Master and Margarita*), Pasternak (*Dr. Zhivago*), Shukshin ("The Cosmos, The Nervous System, A Piece of Lard"), Bitov (*The Pushkin House*), and Rasputin (*Farewell to Matryona*), have dealt with the theme of the generation conflict, heredity, and "the old versus the new" each in his own way. A detailed discussion of this point is outside the scope of the present monograph, but I would suggest that almost all the authors mentioned follow in Turgenev's footsteps in the sense that they tend to show that neither the fathers nor the sons, neither the old nor the new, are without fault, and that in most cases the conflicting parties resemble each other more than they differ.

Fathers and Sons is also a seminal Russian novel in its manifest distrust of reason and logic. Bazarov is undone by his unjustified faith in science, natural law, and intellect. All of Dostoevsky's and Tolstoy's novels are critiques of pure reason. As Reeve points out:

> Tolstoy and Dostoevsky suppose that life is ultimately non-rational and can be dealt with only in non-rational ways—self-denial, love, and so on. Neither writer allows man to become his own god.[59]

Nor does Turgenev, whose greatest novel preceded the major works of those two writers. Nor does any Russian or Soviet writer of international status. A non-rational, anti-heroic view of life is something shared by writers as diverse as Bulgakov, Pasternak, and Solzhenitsyn.

Fathers and Sons also lays down the main lines for the development of the Russian novel by its rejection of extreme characters and its elevation of the middle way. Turgenev, Dostoevsky, and Tolstoy all present us with compelling extreme characters who are ultimately rejected in favor of less interesting, but more enduring, down-to-earth non-heroes. Bazarov is struck down by fate (or commits suicide, depending on one's interpretation), and Arkady and Nikolay are left to multiply and bring forth much fruit. Raskolnikov is endlessly fascinating (as are almost all people when they behave not as they are expected to), but we would much rather have Razumikhin marry into the family. Prince Andrew has glitter and an interesting pallor, but the future belongs to Nikolay. He, Razumikhin, and Arkady are all *positively* mediocre characters whose paramount strength resides *specifically* in their limitations.

In this respect the Russian realistic novel is profoundly antiheroic. It ultimately rejects characters who strive to play the hero. This tendency extends though Turgenev, Dostoevsky, and Tolstoy down to Pasternak. Russian writers have rather consistently answered the repeated calls for positive heroes by creating heroes who are not positive and positive types who are not heroic.[60]

In the preceding pages we have seen, albeit in a cursory manner, that *Fathers and Sons* is a quintessential Russian novel, a central work of nineteenth-century Russian literature. Not only does it reflect what has gone before in the works of Pushkin, Lermontov, and Gogol, but it introduces themes and methods, sometimes only hinting at them, sometimes proclaiming them clearly, that predict the future development of the Russian novel down to the present day.

NOTES FOR CHAPTER I

1. Alexander Boyd, "A Landscape with Figures: Ivan Turgenev and *Fathers and Sons*," *Aspects of the Russian Novel* (Totawa, New Jersey, 1972), 86.

2. T. G. Brazhe, *Tselostnoe izuchenie epicheskogo proizvedeniia* (M, 1964), 19.

3. Joel Blair, "The Architecture of Turgenev's *Fathers and Sons*," *Modern Fiction Studies*, Vol. 19, No. 4 (Winter, 1973-74), 556.

4. See H. Gifford, "Turgenev," in *Nineteenth-Century Russian Literature*, John Fennell, ed., (Berkeley, 1973), 154; Richard Freeborn, *Turgenev: The Novelist's Novelist* (Oxford, 1960), 72.

5. See Freeborn, 72.

6. Vasilii Gippius, "O kompozitsii turgenevskikh romanov," in *Venok Turgenevu* (Odessa, 1919), 25-55. P. G. Pustovoit, *Roman I. S. Turgeneva "Ottsy i deti" i ideinaia bor'ba 60-kh godov* (M, 1960), 207-213, goes out of his way to attack Gippius' study, essentially for no other reason than that it is a product of Russian Formalism. Pustovoit is one of the most prolific and least objective of Soviet specialists on Turgenev.

7. I wish to give credit here to Professor Roger Blakely, who in a course many years ago at Macalester College pointed out the possibility of identifying a comedic structure in *Fathers and Sons*.

8. This is a reduction of what can be found in Northrop Frye, *Anatomy of Criticism* (Princeton, 1957), 43-52, 163-185. The use of the terms "comedic" and "tragedic" is mine, however. I have adopted them in order not to have to speak of the novel's "comic" side.

9. Additional evidence that Arkady's role in *Fathers and Sons* is more than secondary will be brought forth in the chapter on characterization, where I point out that many scenes in the novel are narrated from Arkady's point of view, and in the chapter on *Fathers and Sons* and Turgenev's *oeuvre*, where I note that Arkady's being caught between two women parallels the dilemma of such central heroes in other Turgenev novels as Lavretsky (*A Nest of Gentlefolk*) and Litvinov (*Smoke*). All of this is meant to show that Arkady's role in *Fathers and Sons* is considerably more central than that of the typical secondary character in a Turgenev novel.

10. Gary R. Jahn, "Character and Theme in *Fathers and Sons*," *College Literature*, 4 (1977), 81.

11. James Justus, "*Fathers and Sons*: The Novel as Idyll," *Western Humanities Review*, XV (1961), 262. Justus' comment is additional support for rejecting the notion that the novel's title emphasizes conflict between the generations.

12. The actual title is *Kraft und Stoff*. It first appeared in 1855 and

NOTES FOR CHAPTER I

went through fifteen editions. The first Russian translation appeared in 1860.

13. Alexander Fischler, "The Garden Motif and the Structure of *Fathers and Sons*," *Novel*, 9 (1976), 148.

14. F. R. Reeve, *The Russian Novel* (New York, 1966), 146.

15. Blair, 556.

16. Viktor Shklovskii, *Zametki o proze russkikh klassikov* (M, 1955), 221.

17. Fischler, 244.

18. N. N. Strakhov, "Ottsy i deti," in *O Turgeneve: Russkaia i inostrannaia kritika*, P. P. Pertsov, ed. (M, 1918), 40. Strakhov's article originally appeared in *Vremia*, No. 4 (1862).

19. *Poshly* is a word that does not translate easily. It implies banality, mediocrity, self-satisfied complacency, poor taste, and other allied concepts. The English word "tacky" as it is now used perhaps comes closest to expressing the meaning of the Russian.

20. D. I. Pisarev, "Bazarov," in *Bazarov, Realisty* (M, 1974), 19. Pisarev's article originally appeared in *Russkoe slovo*, No. 3 (March, 1862). All in all, Pisarev's articles on *Fathers and Sons* are among the best in nineteenth-century criticism of the novel.

21. G. A. Bialyi, *Roman Turgeneva "Ottsy i deti"* (M-L, 1963), 66.

22. See Paul Bourget, "Ivan Tourguéniev," in *Nouveaux essais de psychologie contemporaine* (Paris, 1894), 222-224.

23. Boyd, 84.

24. A. Batiuto, *Turgenev-romanist* (L, 1972), 164.

25. I. A. Vinogradov, *Bor'ba za stil'. Sbornik statei* (L, 1937), 199. This is essentially a paraphrase of Strakhov's article on *Fathers and Sons*.

26. Pustovoit, 205, asserts that Arkady's success as an estate manager is ironic in intention, that it is not to be believed. Neither is Pustovoit.

27. A *povest* is a work of fiction longer than a short story and shorter than a novel. In general Turgenev drew a division between his *povesti* and novels (*romany*). The former did not have a social theme, the latter did. A study of Turgenev's correspondence shows, however, that Turgenev was apt to call his novels *povesti* when he was uncertain of their success—as in this case.

28. Gippius, 54.

29. Strakhov, 42-43.

30. Frank F. Seeley, "Theme and Structure in *Fathers and Sons*," *Annali*, Sezione Slava, XII (Naples, 1970), 83-104, was the first to argue that Bazarov's death is perhaps not so much Turgenev's appraisal of the radicals of the 1860s as the only logical outcome of the tragic plot line in which he is embedded.

31. Remarks on the nature of tragedy, unless explicitly stated other-

wise, are based on material to be found in Frye, 35-43, 206-222.

32. Gippius, 53.

33. Iurii Mann, "Bazarov i drugie," *Novyi mir*, 44, x (1968), 247.

34. Frye, 207.

35. Strakhov, 40.

36. Charles R. Bachman, "Tragedy and Self-Deception in Turgenev's *Fathers and Sons*," *Revue des Langues Vivantes* (Brussels), 34, No. 3 (1968), 269.

37. Frye, 208.

38. Freeborn, 121.

39. Fischler, 245.

40. Cf. Turgenev's letter of December 10/22, 1861, to E. E. Lambert, in which apropos of the death of an acquaintance he writes: "But can that really be the end? Can it really be that death is nothing other than life's final departure?—I absolutely do not know what to think—and I can only repeat: 'Happy are those who believe!' " (4, 312).

41. Bachman, 275.

42. Helen Muchnic, *An Introduction to Russian Literature* (New York, 1947), 118.

43. Additional examples of such hesitation about calling the novel a tragedy include V. M. Fisher, "Povest' i roman u Turgeneva," in *Tvorchestvo Turgeneva: Sbornik statei*, I. U. Rozanov and Iu. M. Sokolov, eds. (M, 1920), 37, who calls the novel an elegy, and James Justus, 259, who calls it an idyll. There is a great difference between an elegy and an idyll, of course, and such varied nomenclature only reinforces the thesis that the novel has a dual backbone—tragedy and comedy.

44. Fischler, 244.

NOTES FOR CHAPTER II

1. G. B. Kurliandskaia, *Khudozhestvennyi metod Turgeneva-romanista* (Tula, 1972), 196-197.

2. Kurliandskaia, 158.

3. A. Mazon, *Parizhskie rukopisi I. S. Turgeneva* (M-L, 1931), 59; quoted in A. G. Tseitlin, *Masterstvo Turgeneva-romanista* (M, 1958), 103. The former is a translation of A. Mazon, *Manuscrits parisiens d'Ivan Tourguénev: notices et extraits* (Paris, 1930).

4. Ralph E. Matlaw, "Turgenev's Novels: Civic Responsibility and Literary Predilection," *Harvard Slavic Studies*, IV (1957), 259.

5. Matlaw, 257.

6. A. Batiuto, *Turgenev-romanist* (L, 1972), 205.

7. See Sergei Eizenshtein, "Montazh 1938," *Izbrannye sochineniia*

NOTES FOR CHAPTER II

v 6-i tomakh (M, 1964), II, 156, where Eizenshtein observes that "two pieces of any kind, when placed next to each other, inevitably unite to form a new concept arising out of their juxtaposition as a new quantity." Other relevant works in the same volume include "Vertikal'nyi montazh" (189-268) and "Montazh attraktsionov" (269-273).

8. This is one of the basic theses of George Steiner's *Tolstoy or Dostoevsky: An Essay in the Old Criticism* (New York, 1959).

9. V. M. Fisher, "Povest' i roman u Turgeneva," in *Tvorchestvo Turgeneva: Sbornik statei*, I. U. Rozanov and Iu. M. Sokolov, eds. (M, 1920), 34.

10. Generalizations—some relating to psychology, some to other matters—can be found on 209, 211, 213, 214, 223, 224, 224, 230, 253, 254, 259, 260, 266, 268, 269, 283, 283, 301, 302, 302, 324, 326, 327, 334, 336, 341, 341, 354, 365, 373, and 374. Repeated page numbers indicate the number of generalizations to be found on that page.

11. F. D. Reeve, "Fathers and Children," in *The Russian Novel* (New York, 1966), 135.

12. Matlaw, 258.

13. Fisher, 36.

14. The use of environment for purposes of characterization is hardly original with Turgenev. It occurs often in the works of French realists: Balzac and Stendhal, for instance, both inundate readers with minute depictions of buildings, rooms, toilette, and so on. In Russian literature the device surfaces as early as *Evgeny Onegin*, where Pushkin provides a detailed portrait of Onegin's study. Partly because of the influence of the physiological sketch— French in origin—the technique of characterization via surroundings became standard in the works of Russian authors from the late 1830s on.

15. Batiuto, 201-202.

16. Tseitlin, 118, notes that the strength of Turgenev's portraits lies in their "carefully thought-out juxtapositions." This is fine as far as it goes, but parallels among characters are just as important for characterization.

17. Joel Blair, "The Architecture of Turgenev's *Fathers and Sons*," *Modern Fiction Studies*, Vol. 19, No. 4 (Winter, 1973-74), 559.

18. Blair, 556. Gary Jahn, "Character and Theme in *Fathers and Sons*," *College Literature*, 4 (1977), 80-91, also builds his article around the parallel groupings and regroupings of characters within the novel.

19. The resemblance is not always overlooked. Charles Moser, *Ivan Turgenev* (New York, 1972), 26-27; G. A. Bialyi, *Roman Turgeneva "Ottsy i deti"* (M-L, 1963), 107; Alexander F. Boyd, "A Landscape with Figures: Ivan Turgenev and *Fathers and Sons*," *Aspects of the Russian Novel* (Totawa, New Jersey, 1972), 79; Jahn, 85; and William C. Brumfield, "Bazarov and Rjazanov: The Romantic Archtype in Russian Nihilism," *Slavic and East European Journal*, XXI, 4 (1977), 500, all cite similarities between Bazarov

and Pavel Petrovich. Significantly, there is only one Soviet scholar among this group.

20. Matlaw, 257.
21. Jahn, 85, notes this parallel.
22. Boyd, 79.
23. S. M. Petrov, *I. S. Turgenev: tvorcheskii put'* (M, 1961), 374.
24. Moser, 27.
25. James Justice, "*Fathers and Sons:* The Novel as Idyll," *Western Humanities Review*, XV (1961), 261, writes that "the fathers are associated with the soil, land, and nature." While this is true of Nikolay Petrovich and Vasily Ivanovich, it is decidedly not so with Pavel, who, significantly, is not a father.
26. Michael Nierle, *Die Naturschilderung und ihre Funktionen in Versdichtung und Prosa von I. S. Turgenev* (Verlag Gehlen: Bad Homburg v.d.H., 1969), 249, suggests that Nikolay *and* Pavel love Schiller and Goethe. Similarly, he states that Bazarov *and* Arkady share an enthusiasm for Büchner. Thus, even though on page 248 of his work Nierle says that the problem of the generations in *Fathers and Sons* is one located within generations rather than between them, he goes on to misread the text, attributing a non-existent similarity of views to Pavel and Nikolay, Bazarov and Arkady.
27. In the so-called "Paris manuscript," Bazarov is even more hostile to art. He sees "no use in artists" (449). Turgenev excised the remark, perhaps because it introduces a note of tension into the novel too early.

The so-called "Paris manuscript" is a holding of the Bibliothèque Nationale in Paris. It is Turgenev's final draft (*belovoi avtograf*) of the novel, containing the deletions and additions that Turgenev made after having sent the first draft around for his friends to read and comment on. Therefore it is a valuable document for a study of the novel's gestation. When a photocopy of it was made available to Soviet scholars a minor upheaval ensued in Soviet Turgenev scholarship. One of the more bilious traditions in Soviet scholarship had been that Katkov had castrated the novel before publishing it in *Russkii vestnik*. An examination of the Paris manuscript made it clear that Turgenev himself had made the changes which had so long been attributed to Katkov. Several Soviet critics were thus placed in a rather embarrassing situation. See Charles Moser, *Antinihilism in the Russian Novel of the 1860s* (The Hague, 1964), 82-83, for a more extensive treatment of this laughable development. P. G. Pustovoit, *Roman I. S. Turgeneva "Ottsy i deti" i ideinaia bor'ba 60-kh godov XIX veka* (M, 1960), 108-115, goes on at length about Katkov's brazenness; in a later work, *Roman I. S. Turgeneva "Ottsy i deti": Literaturnyi kommentarii* (M, 1964), Pustovoit admits in a footnote on page 100 that he, Gutiar, Stasov, Brodsky, and Batiuto were dead wrong about Katkov's supposed villainy.

NOTES FOR CHAPTER II

Volume VIII of *PSSP*, 446-478, includes all the variants in the Paris manuscript. In citing those variants the following scheme will be used: the first number indicates the page on which the variant may be found; the second, after a slash, refers to the page of the canonical text to which the variant relates.

28. Blair, 557.
29. Bialyi, 102.
30. Bazarov's attraction to Fenechka undoubtedly has ideological overtones: he can communicate with the peasantry and he readily earns their trust. As we see in his behavior with Fenechka, however, Bazarov easily betrays that trust.
31. *Narod* does not have an exact English equivalent. It is close to the German "Volk." Usually translated as "the people," in works of nineteenth-century Russian literature it refers to the peasantry.
32. Boyd, 79.
33. Seas of ink have been spilled over the question of Bazarov's relation to the peasantry. This is an especially touchy issue for Soviet critics. They interpret Bazarov's last confrontation with the peasants variously. Some argue Turgenev is blinded by his class consciousness in this scene, others admit that Bazarov's doubts about the peasants are an accurate reflection of the attitudes of Pisarev and Nikolay Uspensky. For a detailed treatment of peasants in the works of Turgenev see B. M. Sokolov, "Muzhiki v izobrazhenii Turgeneva," *Tvorchestvo Turgeneva* (Odessa, 1919), 194-233.
34. Turgenev, in "Apropos of *Fathers and Sons*," notes that the radicals attacked him for making Bazarov lose at cards. Had he allowed Bazarov to win, Turgenev is certain that he would have been attacked for portraying Bazarov as a cardsharp (XIV, 100).
35. D. I. Pisarev, "Realisty," in *Bazarov; Realisty* (M, 1974), 109.
36. Bialyi, 77.
37. Bialyi, 77.
38. Blair, 559.
39. Batiuto, 260.
40. Batiuto, 261-263.
41. Richard Freeborn, *Turgenev: The Novelist's Novelist* (Oxford, 1960), 25, notes that the contrast between egoism and altruism is at the root of practically all relationships in Turgenev's novels. Jahn, 89, sees the essential conflicts in the novel as will and intellect versus emotion and sentiment.
42. Professor Helena Goscilo, a colleague, suggests that the lazy cat is identified with the older generation, especially Nikolay, who is covered with dust, while the strutting chicken suggests the younger generation, exemplified by the earringed Peter. This is yet another demonstration of the fact that *Fathers and Sons* yields itself to quite contradictory interpretations.

43. Pisarev, 48, notes that Sitnikov's function in *Fathers and Sons* parallels that of Grushnitsky in Lermontov's *A Hero of Our Time*.

NOTES FOR CHAPTER III

1. The editorial board of *The Contemporary* is an exception to this generalization. One of its editors, M. A. Antonovich, was responsible for the first published review of *Fathers and Sons*, a vituperative article entitled "An Asmodeus of Our Time," which appeared in the third issue of *The Contemporary* for 1862. In his review Antonovich opined that Bazarov was a caricature of the younger generation.

2. Pustovoit, *Roman I. S. Turgeneva "Ottsy i deti" i ideinaia bor'ba 60-kh godov XIX veka* (M, 1960), 128. This work will henceforth be referred to as *Ideinaia bor'ba*.

3. The same is true of Rudin in Turgenev's eponymous novel.

4. Characters in *Rudin* react similarly strongly to Rudin.

5. Many of Bazarov's enigmatic qualities are shared by Dostoevsky's Stavrogin *(The Possessed)* and Lermontov's Pechorin. Later in the chapter Bazarov's links with the Romantic hero are traced.

6. See Turgenev's letter to Sluchevsky (4, 387).

7. Helen Muchnic, *An Introduction to Russsian Literature* (New York, 1964), 116.

8. Ralph Matlaw, "Turgenev's Novels and *Fathers and Sons*," in Ivan Turgenev, *Fathers and Sons: The Author on the Novel, Contemporary Reactions, Essays in Criticism*, ed. with a substantially new translation by Ralph Matlaw (New York, 1966), 277.

9. Joel Blair, "The Architecture of Turgenev's *Fathers and Sons*," *Modern Fiction Studies*, Vol. 19, No. 4 (Winter, 1973-74), 557.

10. Ralph Matlaw, "Turgenev's Novels: Civic Responsibility and Literary Predilection," *Harvard Slavic Studies*, IV (1957), 258.

11. P. G. Pustovoit, *Roman I. S. Turgeneva "Ottsy i deti"* (M, 1964), 93.

12. See letter to Katkov, 11/23 January, 1862 (4, 324).

13. Muchnic, 116.

14. Edmund Wilson, "Turgenev and the Life-Giving Drop," *A Window on Russia* (New York, 1972), 119-120.

15. Eva Kagan-Kans, *Hamlet and Don Quixote: Turgenev's Ambivalent Vision* (The Hague, 1975), 33.

16. A. Batiuto, *Turgenev-romanist* (L, 1972), 261.

17. G. M. Fridlender and A. I. Batiuto, "Ottsy i deti," *Istoriia russkogo romana* (M-L, 1962), I, 512.

18. Iuri Mann, "Bazarov i drugie," *Novyi mir,* 44, x (1968), 243.

19. Freeborn, 68, 126. Gary Jahn, "Character and Theme in *Fathers and Sons,*" *College Literature,* 4 (1977), 89, says much the same thing in noting that in Turgenev's novel "true happiness, represented by all the positive human characteristics in full degree, is shown to be logically impossible."

20. Turgenev conceived the idea for the essay in 1847, but it was not finished and published until 1860. See VIII, 553-555.

21. Turgenev wrote of Belinsky' "Belinsky was as much an idealist as a negationist; he negated in the name of his ideal" (XIV, 42).

22. Turgenev said of Belinsky that his "knowledge was not vast; he knew little and there is nothing surprising about that" (XIV, 29).

23. Pustovoit, *Roman Turgeneva,* 142-146, obviously senses this, because he goes on at length about the high seriousness of the frog episodes.

24. E. Lampert, *Sons Against Fathers* (Oxford, 1965), 243, writing of Dobroliubov, one of the commonly adduced historical prototypes for Bazarov, notes that "he [Dobroliubov] is fairly typical of those whose rejection of error is more convincing and more meaningful than the positive formula in which they try to define what they believe."

25. There is a passage in the Paris manuscript that sounds like an ironic echo of this section of Turgenev's essay. In the canonical text, Odintsova remarks to Bazarov apropos of her aunt: "But now I hear my aunt coming to take tea; we must spare her ears" (278). The Paris manuscript, however, appends: "She's old, but all the same she needn't be destroyed" (458).

An examination of the Paris manuscript reveals that in the first draft Odintsova occasionally takes issue with Bazarov's pronouncements, and in such a way as to make him look rather silly. Turgenev subsequently removed all such passages.

26. Pustovoit, *Roman I. S. Turgeneva,* 135, suggests that Turgenev rejected the epigraph because Bazarov clearly does not represent strength without content. Pustovoit's work bristles with similar insights.

N. A. Ostrovskaia, "Vospominaniia o Turgeneve," in *Turgenevskii sbornik,* Piksanov, ed. (Petrograd, 1916), 75, claims that Turgenev said to her: "We, the people of the 1840s, had content without will, but they [the men of the 1860s] have will without content."

27. Earlier scholarship linked Bazarov's gloomy meditations on nature and the universe to Schopenhauer's philosophy. Batiuto, 62-83, discusses the tradition and goes on to demonstrate beyond the shadow of a doubt that Bazarov's musings are reworkings of certain of Pascal's *Pensées.*

28. Lampert, 101, notes that Chernyshevsky, another commonly suggested prototype for Bazarov, complained in his diary of a "tendency to Hamletism." Scholars (and there are several) who claim that Bazarov's Hamletism is an historical inaccuracy ignore the facts.

29. H. Gifford, "Turgenev," in John Fennell, ed., *Nineteenth-Century Russian Literature* (Berkeley, 1973), 157.

30. Significant German criticism of *Hamlet* is neatly anthologized in William Shakespeare, *Hamlet,* ed. Horace Howard Furness (New York, 1963), Vol. II. Of particular relevance here are the excerpt from Goethe's *Wilhelm Meisters Lehrjahre* Book V, and A. W. Schlegel's "Lectures on Art and Dramatic Literature."

31. See VIII, 558.

32. Marina Ledkovsky, *The Other Turgenev: From Romanticism to Symbolism* (Wurzberg, 1973). An additional recent work on Turgenev's ties with Romanticism is Antoni Semczuk, *Iwan Turgeniew i ruch literacki w Rosji w latach 1834-1855* (Wroclaw, 1968).

33. See Alexander Fischler, "The Garden Motif and the Structure of Turgenev's *Fathers and Sons,"* *Novel,* 9 (1976), 246; and William C. Brumfield, "Bazarov and Rjazanov: The Romantic Archetype in Russian Nihilism," *Slavic and East European Journal,* XXI, No. 4 (1977), 495-501. Both of these authors treat Bazarov as a Romantic hero.

34. Mann, 247.

35. C. H. van Schooneveld, "Gogol' and the Romantics," in *Essays in Honor of Kiril Taranovsky,* Roman Jakobson, C. H. van Schooneveld, and Dean S. Worth, eds. (The Hague, 1973), 481.

36. Mario Praz, *The Romantic Agony,* trans. Angus Davidson (New York, 1951), 57.

37. To compensate for this lack K. Chernyshev, *Lishnie liudi i zhenskie tipy v romanax i povestiakh I. S. Turgeneva* (M-St. P, 1913), 128-130, provides a touching childhood and university education for Bazarov.

38. Bialyi, *Roman Turgeneva "Ottsy i deti,"* 37-38.

39. F. D. Reeve, "Fathers and Children," *The Russian Novel* (New York, 1966), 135.

40. Matlaw, "Turgenev's Novels: Civic Responsibility," 261.

41. George Lord Byron, "Lara," *Works of Lord Byron* (New York, 1966), III, 321.

42. Batiuto, 200, points out that most of Turgenev's heroes are laconic. This fact does not make Bazarov's silence any less enigmatic.

43. Bazarov's remarks are taken almost literally from Pomialovsky's *Molotov.* See Pustovoit, *Ideinaia bor'ba,* 159.

44. Praz, 68.

45. Matlaw, "Turgenev's Novels," 274-275. In the same article, 272, Matlaw points out that Meierkhold wanted to cast Mayakovsky in the role of Bazarov in a projected stage version of *Fathers and Sons.* The appropriateness of Meierkhold's choice is stunning.

46. Praz, 74.

NOTES FOR CHAPTER III

47. See pp. 65-66 of the present work.

48. N. A. Ostrovskaia, "Vospominaniia N. A. Ostrovskoi," in *I. S. Turgenev v vospominaniiakh sovremennikov i ego pis'makh* (M, 1924), I, 68.

49. Pustovoit, *Ideinaia bor'ba*, 130, points out—facts to the contrary— that no "real" man of the 1860s would have been as shattered by an unsuccessful love affair as Bazarov is. Lampert, *Sons Against Fathers*, shows that Chernyshevsky, Dobroliubov, and Pisarev all had extraordinarily painful involvements with women.

50. Praz, 31, observes that beauty and death were looked upon as sisters by the Romantics.

51. Translation Matlaw, "Turgenev's novels," 277-278. That Turgenev's characterization of Bazarov owes a debt to Byron is suggested by Dostoevsky in *The Possessed*, where Stepan Verkhovensky calls Bazarov "some sort of murky mixture of Gogol's Nozdrev and Byron." See Chapter VI of the present work for more on the links between *Fathers and Sons* and *The Possessed*.

52. Henri Granjard, *Ivan Tourguénev et les courants politiques et sociaux de son temps* (Paris, 1953), 279. A. I. Batiuto, "K voprosu o zamysle Ottsov i detei," in *I. S. Turgenev. 1818-1883-1958. Stat'i i materialy*, M. P. Alexeev, ed. (Orel, 1960), 85-86, illuminates the portrait of Marino from quite another point of view. He uses letters and memoirs to show that Marino, with its trees that have not taken and pond filled with precious little water, is a fictionalized portrait of Fet's incredibly unattractive estate, Stepanovka. S. M. Petrov, *I. S. Turgenev. Tvorcheskii put'* (M, 1961), 357, argues that the description of Marino is meant to underscore the critical state of the old culture, i.e., the gentry.

53. Bialyi, 40-41.

54. Consultations with several native speakers of Russian confirm that Pavel's phrase is unidiomatic *because* it is hypercorrect.

55. Not *Galignani's Messager*, as the notes to Volume VIII indicate (613).

56. Gifford, 154.

57. See Freeborn, 72; Irving Howe, *Politics and the Novel* (London, 1961), 130-131; I. A. Vinogradov, *Bor'ba za stil': sbornik statei* (L, 1937), 197; V. M. Fisher, "Povest' i roman u Turgeneva," in *Tvorchestvo Turgeneva: sbornik statei*, I. U. Rozanov and Iu. M. Sokolov, eds. (M, 1920), 34.

58. Blair, 561.

59. See Chapter I of the present work.

60. In addition, it may well be that the duel in *Fathers and Sons* is an echo of Turgenev's near-duel with Tolstoy. Batiuto, "K voprosu...", 87-93, notes that at the time when Turgenev and Tolstoy came close to a duel, they were both guests of Fet at Stepanovka, which may be the prototype for

Marino (see note 52). Batiuto marshals his data quite convincingly to show that *Fathers and Sons* was only about half completed when Turgenev arrived at Stepanovka. (At Spasskoe he gave the manuscript to Tolstoy to read. The latter fell asleep over it, but that is another story.) Thus, argues Batiuto, it is quite possible that the idea of having Bazarov and Pavel fight a duel may have grown out of Turgenev's personal experience. Batiuto goes on to argue that Tolstoy is one of Bazarov's prototypes. For more on this point, see pp. 95-98 of the present work.

61. Batiuto, *Turgenev-romanist*, 203.

62. Alexander F. Boyd, "A Landscape with Figures: Ivan Turgenev and *Fathers and Sons*," *Aspects of the Russian Novel* (Totawa, New Jersey, 1972), 85.

63. Fisher, 34.

64. Boyd, 84.

65. It would seem that many of the great Russian writers of the nineteenth century just were not very good at arithmetic. R. F. Christian, "The Passage of Time in *Anna Karenina*," *Slavonic and East European Review* (January 1967), 207-210, demonstrates that in *Anna Karenina* ages are muddled, distances do not tally, and the day on which the novel begins is both a Thursday and a Friday. Dostoevsky's notebooks *(Neizdannyi Dostoevskii* [M, 1971]), which are chock full of columns and columns of financial calculations, show that the author whose Underground Man said that "sometimes two plus two equals five is also a very nice thing" had great difficulty in adding a simple column of figures: mistakes abound.

66. Kagan-Kans, 50.

67. Surely Turgenev's portraits of predatory or infernal women are not unrelated to his own experiences with Pauline Viardot.

68. Blair, 560.

69. Kagan-Kans, 51.

70. Kagan-Kans, 51.

71. See Fisher, 31, 32; Batiuto, 371.

72. M. A. Petrovskii, "Tainstvennoe u Turgeneva," in *Tvorchestvo Turgeneva: sbornik statei*, I. U. Rozanov and Iu. M. Sokolov, eds. (M, 1920), 88.

73. Kagan-Kans, 276-277, notes that passion and fire are linked in Turgenev's use of imagery.

74. Ralph Matlaw, "Turgenev's Novels and *Fathers and Sons*," in Ivan Turgenev, *Fathers and Sons: The Author on the Novel, Contemporary Criticism*, ed. with a substantially new translation by Ralph Matlaw (New York, 1966), 276-277. As Matlaw goes on to suggest in his essay, Tolstoy in his novels does not need to compress time in order to show its capacity for altering people.

NOTES FOR CHAPTER IV

  1. A standard work on the rift is V. Evgen'iev-Maksimov, *N. A. Nekrasov i ego sovremenniki* (M, 1930). Henri Granjard, *Ivan Tourguénev et les courants politiques et sociaux de son temps* (Paris, 1953), 257-298, also summarizes the major events leading up to the break.

  2. *Raznochinets* is a word that is not easily translated into English. It refers to a non-gentry member of the Russian intelligentsia in the nineteenth century. Belinsky was a *raznochinets,* and by the 1860s the ranks of the radicals were filled with *raznochintsy.* For a detailed discussion see Martin Malia, "What Is the Intelligentsia," in *The Russian Intelligentsia,* ed. Richard Pipes (New York, 1961), 1-18.

  3. Gore Vidal, *Matters of Fact and Fiction* (New York, 1977), 28, observes that the problem with much contemporary British and American literature is that too many writers mistake the university for the universe.

  4. Malia, 18. Alexander Fischler, "The Garden Motif and the Structure of Turgenev's *Fathers and Sons," Novel,* 9 (1976), 250-251, suggests that Bazarov's father's reliance on Classical allusions is part of the overall Classical "architecture" revealed in the novel. Malia's and Fischler's contrasting analyses of the Bazarov family's speech are a prime example of Turgenev's ability to wed topicality to universal concerns in the novel.

  5. Turgenev's notes on the first performance of Meyerbeer's *Le Prophète* (V, 347-352) are far ahead of their time in suggesting that the opera is rather a bore and that Meyerbeer is not a first-class composer.

  6. See notes: VIII, 590-591.

  7. A. I. Batiuto, "K voprosu o zamysle *Ottsov i detei,"* in *I. S. Turgenev. 1818-1883-1958. Stat'i i materialy,* M. P. Alekseev, ed. (Orel, 1960), 77-96.

  8. Iurii Mann, "Bazarov i drugie," *Novyi mir,* 44, x (1968), 240.

  9. See "Apropos of *Fathers and Sons,"* XIV, 97.

  10. N. N. Strakhov, "Ottsy i deti," in *O Turgeneve: russkaia i inostrannaia kritika,* P. P. Pertsov, ed. (M, 1918), 32.

  11. A. I. Polovtsev, *Russkie pisateli o literaturnom trude,* II (M, 1955), 753. Cited in P. G. Pustovoit, *Roman I. S. Turgeneva "Ottsy i deti": Literaturnyi kommentarii* (M, 1964), 13. Pustovoit's work will henceforth be referred to as *Roman.*

  12. Isaiah Berlin, *Fathers and Children* (Oxford, 1972), 24; Granjard, 300; notes to "Apropos of *Fathers and Sons,"* XII, 467.

  13. N. M. Chernov, "Ob odnom znakomstve I. S. Turgeneva," *Voprosy literatury,* No. 8 (1961), 188-193, throws considerable doubt on the credibility of Polovtsev's version.

  14. See Pustovoit, *Roman,* 89-90.

  15. N. A. Ostrovskaia, "Vospominaniia o Turgeneve," in *Turgenevskii sbornik,* Piksanov, ed. (Petrograd, 1916), 79.

16. See note 13.

17. W. Edgerton, "I. S. Turgenev i spornyi vopros o Iakushkinykh," *Russkaia literatura*, No. 1 (1967), 149-154. Professor Edgerton's totally persuasive article seems to have escaped the attention of some Turgenev scholars. Galina Vinnikova, *Turgenev i Rossiia* (M, 1971), 174, identifies Yakushkin as a prototype for Bazarov.

18. Berlin, 24; Granjard, 300.

19. Translation by David Magarshack, in Ivan Turgenev, *Literary Reminiscences and Autobiographical Fragments*, trans. with intro. by Magarshack (New York, 1958), 193-194.

20. Translation Magarshack, 196.

21. Batiuto is an exception, as usual. In "K voprosu...," 78, he suggests that Turgenev's observations of Belinsky played a role in the creation of Bazarov.

22. Berlin, 25.

23. Malia, 18, points out that the principal foreign language of the *raznochintsy* was Latin.

24. S. M. Petrov, *I. S. Turgenev: tvorcheskii put'* (M, 1961), 37, suggests that Bazarov's speech is intended as a reaction to the grandiloquence of the men of the 1840s.

25. Berlin, 25.

26. Pustovoit, *Roman*, 134.

27. Cited in Pustovoit, *Roman*, 40.

28. Richard Freeborn, *Turgenev: The Novelist's Novelist* (Oxford, 1960), 40.

29. Petrov, 363.

30. See G. A. Bialyi, *Roman Turgeneva "Ottsy i deti"* (M-L, 1963), 158-159.

31. N. A. Dobroliubov, "Nikolai Nikolaevich Stankevich," *Sobranie sochinenii v 9-i tomakh* (M-L, 1962), II, 394-395.

32. See A. Batiuto, *Turgenev-romanist* (L, 1972), 228, for the origins of this tradition. Further references to this work will be indicated by Batiuto's name without a title.

33. Batiuto, 230-232.

34. See N. G. Chernyshevskii, "Vospominaniia ob otnosheniiakh Turgeneva k Dobroliubovu i o razryve druzhby mezhdu Turgenevym i Nekrasovym," in *I. S. Turgenev v vospominaniiakh sovremennikov* (M, 1969), Vol. I, 356, for Dobroliubov's legendary statement to Turgenev: "Ivan Sergeevich, I'm bored talking to you, let's stop talking [to each other]."

35. E. Lampert, *Sons Against Fathers*, (Oxford, 1965), 254.

36. See Chernyshevskii, 354-358; Granjard, 298; Turgenev's letters to Shcherban' (Volume 4 of Letters).

37. Chernyshevskii, 366.
38. Granjard, 309.
39. See VIII, 577-578.
40. See VIII, 616.
41. Batiuto, 114.
42. See VIII, 621.
43. See Petrov, 366-371; P. G. Pustovoit, *Roman I. S. Turgeneva "Ottsy i deti" i ideinaia bor'ba 60-kh godov XIX veka* (M, 1960), 53-54. This work will henceforth be referred to as *Ideinaia bor'ba*.
44. Petrov, 392; Pustovoit, *Ideinaia bor'ba*, 54.
45. Petrov, 386.
46. See N. K. Piksanov, "Velikoe nasledie Turgeneva," in *I. S. Turgenev: materialy i issledovaniia*, N. L. Brodskii, ed. (Orel, 1940), 74, where Piksanov treats Bazarov's anti-estheticism as a parody of Pisarev's views.
47. Batiuto, 223.
48. See D. I Pisarev, "Bazarov," in *Bazarov; Realisty* (M, 1974), 33. Pisarev's article was first published in *Russkoe slovo*, No. 3 (March 1862).
49. Charles A. Moser, *Antinihilism in the Russian Novel of the 1860s* (The Hague, 1964), 288.
50. See Petrov, 392; Bialyi, 48-49.
51. See note 7.
52. Batiuto, "K voprosu...," 82.
53. Batiuto, "K voprosu...," 84.
54. V. I. Lenin, "Lev Tolstoi, kak zerkalo russkoi revoliutsii," in *V. I. Lenin o L. N. Tolstom* (M, 1969), 17-23.
55. Pustovoit, *Roman*, 37-37.
56. Petrov, 384.
57. Bialyi, 92.
58. G. Bialyi, *Turgenev i russkii realizm* (M-L, 1962), 167.
59. T. G. Brazhe, *Tselostnoe izuchenie epicheskogo proizvedeniia* (M, 1964), 78.
60. Pustovoit, *Roman*, 176.
61. Strakhov, 32.
62. F. D. Reeve, "Fathers and Children," *The Russian Novel* (New York, 1966), 135.
63. See Mann, 237.
64. See Batiuto, 227.
65. Granjard, 265.
66. Granjard, 308. The refusal to recognize any principles brings Bazarov's worldview closest to that of Pisarev, who similarly rejected all *a priori* assumptions, principles.
67. Irving Howe, "Turgenev: The Politics of Hesitation," *Politics and*

the Novel (London, 1961), 130.

68. Dale E. Peterson, *The Clement Vision: Poetic Realism in Turgenev and James* (Port Washington, New York, 1975), 80.

69. I wish to thank my colleague, Professor Helena Goscilo, for pointing out to me this underlying consistency in Bazarov's worldview.

70. Herzen's "Eshche raz Bazarov," *Sobranie sochinenii v 30-i tomakh* (M, 1963), Vol. XX, kn. 1, 335-350, is largely an outraged rebuttal of the notion that Pavel and Nikolay are the best that the generation of the 1840s has to offer.

71. See page 70 of the present work.

72. Pustovoit, *Ideinaia bor'ba,* 34, points out that *The Russian Messenger,* the journal in which *Fathers and Sons* first appeared, also oriented itself toward England.

73. Granjard, 305.

74. Granjard, 305.

75. Freeborn, 72.

76. Howe, 131.

77. Howe, 131.

78. I. A. Vinogradov, *Bor'ba za stil': sbornik statei* (L, 1937), 197.

79. See page 83 of the present work.

80. In this respect Bazarov is as ineffectual a hero as Rudin, and it is not altogether surprising that Turgenev's friend on the Isle of Wight (see page 86) had the reaction to Turgenev's plans for the novel that he did.

81. Moser, *Antinihilism,* 83.

NOTES FOR CHAPTER V

1. D. S. Mirsky, *A History of Russian Literature from Its Beginnings to 1900,* ed. Francis J. Whitfield (New York, 1953), 203.

2. Mirsky, 203.

3. V. M. Fisher, "Povest' i roman u Turgeneva," in *Tvorchestvo Turgeneva: sbornik statei,* I. U. Rozanov and Iu. M. Sokolov, eds. (M, 1920), 3.

4. Eva Kagan-Kans, *Hamlet and Don Quixote: Turgenev's Ambivalent Vision* (The Hague, 1975), 9.

5. See Kagan-Kans, 9.

6. Mirsky, 200.

7. For a discussion of the origin of this tradition see A. Batiuto, *Turgenev-romanist* (L, 1972), 241-242.

8. Batiuto, 241-242.

9. Batiuto, 261.

10. Kagan-Kans, 33.

NOTES FOR CHAPTER V

11. Batiuto, 260-262.
12. G. A. Bialyi, *Roman Turgeneva "Ottsy i deti"* (M-L, 1963), 39.
13. Kagan-Kans, 10.
14. See Kagan-Kans, 9.
15. See the next chapter, page 123, for a detailed treatment of this point.
16. Vasilii Gippius, "O kompozitsii turgenevskikh romanov," in *Venok Turgenevu: sbornik statei* (Odessa, 1919), 52.
17. Mirsky, 203-204.
18. See page 36 for an elaboration on this point.
19. In fact the original plan for *Fathers and Sons* has not survived, but it seems highly unlikely that the plan could have included any more of a thesis than the one implied in the novel's projected epigraph (see page 63).
20. Richard Freeborn, *Turgenev: The Novelist's Novelist* (Oxford, 1960), 55.
21. See Kagan-Kans, 57-59, 75-77.
22. Freeborn, 43.
23. See pages 22-24 for a discussion of the virtues of Nikolay's and Arkady's married lives.
24. See Freeborn, 55.
25. P. G. Pustovoit, *Roman I. S. Turgeneva "Ottsy i deti" i ideinaia bor'ba 60-kh godov XIX veka* (M, 1960), 214.
26. G. M. Fridlender and A. I. Batiuto, *"Ottsy i deti,"* in *Istoriia russkogo romana* (M-L, 1962), I, 495.
27. Alexander F. Boyd, "A Landscape with Figures: Ivan Turgenev and *Fathers and Sons,"* in *Aspects of the Russian Novel* (Totawa, New Jersey, 1972), 84.
28. Mirsky, 202.
29. G. Bialyi, *Turgenev i russkii realizm* (M-L, 1962), 158.
30. Boyd, 84.
31. Kagan-Kans, 42.
32. Mirsky, 204.
33. See pages 58-60 on Bazarov's dynamism.
34. Gippius, 26.
35. Gippius, 26.
36. Gippius, 33-34.
37. Gippius, 35.
38. Virginia M. Burns, "The Structure of the Plot in *Otcy i deti,"* *Russian Literature*, 6 (1974), 33-53; Alexander Fischler, "The Garden Motif and the Structure of Turgenev's *Fathers and Sons*," *Novel*, 9 (1976), 243-255.
39. Burns, 53.

40. Fischler, 244.

NOTES FOR CHAPTER VI

1. See VIII, 621. In the epilogue the flowers on Bazarov's grave speak "not only of the great calm of 'indifferent' nature" (402). The last four lines of Pushkin's poem read: "And at the entrance to the grave/ May young life play,/ And indifferent nature/ Shine with eternal beauty."
2. L. V. Pumpianskii, "Romany Turgeneva i roman *Nakanune*: istoriko-literaturnyi ocherk," in I. S. Turgenev, *Sochineniiia v 12-i tomakh* (M, 1928-1934), VI, 9-26.
3. Chapter III, v.
4. A. Batiuto, *Turgenev-romanist* (L, 1972), 272-273.
5. Chapter VI, v.
6. See page 66 of the present work.
7. Batiuto, 378-384, discusses this whole question.
8. See Charles A. Moser, *Ivan Turgenev* (New York, 1972), 40.
9. D. I. Pisarev, "Bazarov," *Bazarov; Realisty* (M, 1974), 48; "Realisty," *op. cit.*, 115.
10. F. D. Reeve, "Fathers and Children," *The Russian Novel* (New York, 1966), 134.
11. Vladimir Nabokov, "Translator's Foreword," in Mihail Lermontov, *A Hero of Our Time*, trans. Vladimir Nabokov (New York, 1958), xi-xii.
12. G. M. Fridlender and A. I. Batiuto, *"Ottsy i deti,"* in *Istoriia russkogo romana* (M-L, 1962), I, 509-510. See also Batiuto, 370-371.
13. In "Apropos of *Fathers and Sons*" Turgenev writes: "No matter how modest I may be in my opinion of my gifts—I nevertheless considered and consider the composition of a lampoon, a 'pasquile,' beneath them, unworthy of them" (XIV, 99). See A. G. Tseitlin, *Masterstvo Turgeneva-romanista* (M, 1958), 110, on Turgenev's hostility toward Tolstoyan repetition.
14. Batiuto, 371.
15. Chapter II, xxxii.
16. Milton Ehre, *Oblomov and His Creater: The Life and Art of Ivan Goncharov* (Princeton, 1973), 262.
17. Vasilii Gippius, "O kompozitsii turgenevskikh romanov," in *Venok Turgenevu: sbornik statei* (Odessa, 1919), 53.
18. See Ralph E. Matlaw, "Turgenev's Novels: Civic Responsibility and Literary Predilection," *Harvard Slavic Studies*, IV (1957), 254.
19. Charles A. Moser, *Antinihilism in the Russian Novel of the 1860s* (The Hague, 1964), 106-107.
20. See Henri Granjard, *Ivan Tourguénev et les courants politiques et sociaux de son temps* (Paris, 1966), 318; also S. M. Petrov, *I. S. Turgenev:*

tvorcheskii put' (M, 1961), 394. Batiuto, 114, suggests that the structure of *What Is to Be Done?* is derivative of that of Turgenev's *On the Eve*.

21. The appendix to Moser's work contains handy synopses of these and lesser works which I have not mentioned.

22. See B. M. Eikhenbaum, *Lev Tolstoi* (L, 1928/31), II, 193-195.

23. See Fyodor Dostoevsky, *The Notebooks for "The Possessed,"* ed. and intro. Edward Wasiolek, trans. Victor Terras (Chicago, 1968), 173, note.

24. The other was Botkin. See letter to K. K. Sluchevskii, April 14/26, 1862 (12, 380).

25. M. Bakhtin, *Problemy poetiki Dostoevskogo* (M, 1972), 37-38. Translated by R. W. Rotsel: Mikhail Bakhtin, *Problems of Dostoevsky's Poetics* (Ann Arbor, 1973), 18.

26. Bialyi, 42.

27. Bakhtin, 130-131. Translation Rotsel, 63.

28. Matlaw, 254.

29. Bialyi, 43.

30. Bialyi, 42.

31. Richard Freeborn, *Turgenev: The Novelist's Novelist* (Oxford, 1960), 124.

32. Bialyi, 42.

33. *The Possessed* was initially published serially in the January 1871-December 1872 issues of *The Russian Messenger*.

34. See F. M. Dostoevskii, *Pis'ma,* ed. A. S. Dolinin (M, 1930), II, 333.

35. Iuri Nikol'skii, *Turgenev i Dostoevskii: istoriia odnoi vrazhdy* (Sofia, 1921); A. S. Dolinin, "Turgenev v 'Besakh'," in *F. M. Dostoevskii: stat'i i materialy*, ed. A. S. Dolinin (M-L, 1924), II, 119-138; I. S. Zil'bershtein, "Vstrecha Dostoevskogo s Turgenevym v Badene v 1867 g.," in *Dostoevskii i Turgenev: perpepiska* (L, 1928), 143-187.

36. M. S. Al'tman, "Etiudy po Dostoevskomu," *Izvestiia An SSSR*, seriia literatury i iazyka (1963), Vol. XXII, vyp. 6.

37. The commentary and annotations to the recent Academy edition of *The Possessed* (see following note for full citation) mention *Smoke* (XII, 167), "Apropos of *Fathers and Sons*" (XII, 167), "Recollections of Belinsky" (XII, 167), *Fathers and Sons* (XII, 173), "A Few Remarks about Russian Agriculture and the Russian Peasant" (XII, 287), *A Nest of Gentlefolk* (XII, 287), "The Execution of Traupmann" (XII, 291), "Enough" (XII, 309), and "Phantoms" (XII, 309).

38. See F. M. Dostoevskii, *Polnoe sobranie sochinenii* (L, 1972-   ), Vol. XII, 167. Further references to this source will be indicated by a volume and page number within the text.

39. N. F. Budanova, "Problema 'ottsov' i 'detei' v romane 'Besy,' " in *Dostoevskii: materialy i issledovaniia*, G. M. Fridlender, ed., (L, 1974), 164-

NOTES FOR CHAPTER VI

188; also Dostoevskii, Vol. XII, 174-175.

40. Budanova, 166-167.

41. See note 8.

42. References to Bazarov in the notebooks may be found in Vol. XI, pp. 67, 71, and 72.

43. See Dostoevskii, V, 59. The full context of this phrase is quoted later in this chapter.

44. Herzen, "Very Dangerous!!", Vol. XIV, 116.

45. As noted in Chapter III, the characterization of both Bazarov and Stavrogin owes more than a little to Lermontov's Pechorin.

46. Cf. Lermontov's Grushnitsky.

47. See note 34.

48. See Dostoevskii, *Pis'ma*, Vol. I, 343, 352.

49. See note 35.

50. See note 36.

51. See note 36.

52. For the most balanced study to date for the relations between Turgenev and Viardot, see Leonard Schapiro, *Ivan Turgenev: His Life and Times* (New York, 1978).

53. There is an additional and, in this case, ex post facto parallel between Stepan Verkhovensky and Turgenev. In *The Possessed* we learn that one of the factors contributing to renewed interest in Verkhovensky is the false report of his death (X, 20). Curiously, in early 1872 Turgenev's death was also falsely reported in a number of European journals and newspapers (9, 212).

54. Discussions of Dostoevsky's complex attitude toward Bazarov include Bialyi, *op. cit.*; K. I. Tiun'kin, "Bazarov glazami Dostoevskogo," in *Dostoevskii i ego vremia*, ed. by V. G. Bazanov and G. M. Fridlender (L, 1971), 108-119; and A. I. Batiuto, "Priznaki velikogo serdtsa," in *Russkaia literatura*, No. 2 (1977), 21-37. Unfortunately, none of these articles mentions Bazarov in the context of *The Possessed*.

55. Budanova (XII, 176) argues, for instance, that the links between *Fathers and Sons* and *The Possessed* grow weaker after the February notebooks, a view that does not hold up under careful analysis.

56. Matlaw, 276.

57. Letter from a colleague, Professor Helena Goscilo.

58. George Steiner, *Tolstoy or Dostoevsky: An Essay in the Old Criticism* (New York, 1959), 145.

59. Reeve, 151.

60. Soviet critics would take indignant exception to this, citing scores of positive heroes in the classics of Socialist Realism. Such heroes are positive and heroic and bear no resemblance to any living being on land or sea.

SELECTED BIBLIOGRAPHY

TURGENEV'S WORKS:

Turgenev, Ivan Sergeevich. *Sochineniia v 12-i tomakh,* eds. K. I. Khalabaev and B. M. Eikhenbaum. M. 1928-1934.
Turgenev, Ivan Sergeevich. *Sobranie sochinenii v 11-i tomakh,* ed. N. L. Brodskii. M. 1949.
Turgenev, Ivan Sergeevich. *Polnoe sobranie sochinenii i pisem v 28-i tomakh.* M-L. 1960-1968.

WORKS DEALING WITH *FATHERS AND SONS*:

Note: In the case of monographs, page numbers refer to passages that deal with *Fathers and Sons.*

Aikhenval'd, Iu. *Siluety russkikh pisatelei.* M. 1909, 154-167.
Alekseev, M. P. "K istorii slova 'nigilizm'," *Sbornik statei v chest' akademika A. I. Sobolevskogo.* L. 1928.
Al'tman, M. S. "Etiudy po Dostoevskomu," *Izvestiia AN SSSR,* Seriia literatury i iazyka, Vol. XXII, vyp. 6, 1963, 495-496.
Annenkov, P. V. *Literaturnye vospominaniia.* M. 1960, 538.
Antonovich, M. A. "Asmodei nashego vremeni," *Sovremennik,* No. 3, 1862.
Arkhipov, V. "K tvorcheskoi istorii romana I. S. Turgeneva *Ottsy i deti,*" *Russkaia literatura,* No. 1, 1958, 132-136.
Arkhipov, V. "Protiv teorii 'edinogo potoka'," *Russkaia literatura,* No. 2, 1959, 95-130.
Azadovskii, M. K. "Ob odnom siuzhetnom sovpadenii ('Smert' ateista' v romane Omulevskogo i u Ippolita Tena)," *Akademiku N. Ia. Marru.* M-L. 1935, 589.
Bachman, Charles R. "Tragedy and Self-Deception in Turgenev's *Fathers and Sons,*" *Revue des Langues Vivantes* (Brussels), Vol. XXXIV, No. 3, 269-276.
Batiuto, A. I. "K voprosu o proiskhozhdenii slova 'nigilizm' v romane I. S. Turgeneva *Ottsy i deti,*" *Izvestiia AN SSSR,* Otdelenie literatury i iazyka, Vol. XII, vyp. 6, 1953, 520-525.
Batiuto, A. I. "K voprosu o zamysle *Ottsov i detei,*" *I. S. Turgenev. 1818-1883-1958. Stat'i i materialy,* ed. M. P. Alekseev. Orel, 1960, 77-96.
Batiuto, A. I. "Parizhskaia rukopis' romana I. S. Turgeneva *Ottsy i deti,*" *Russkaia literatura,* No. 4, 1961, 57-78.

Batiuto, A. I. "Priznaki velikogo serdtsa," *Russkaia literatura,* No. 2 (1977), 21-37.
Batiuto, A. I. "Strukturno-zhanrovoe svoeobrazie romanov Turgeneva 50-kh— nachala 60-kh godov," *Problemy realizma russkoi literatury XIX veka.* M-L. 1961.
Batiuto, A. I. "Turgenev i B. Paskal'," *Russkaia literatura,* No. 1, 1964, 153-162.
Batiuto, A. I. *Turgenev-romanist.* L. 1972.
Bel'chikov, N. "3 otdelenie i roman *Ottsy i deti,"* *Dokumenty po istorii literatury i obshchestvennosti.* Vyp. II. M-Pg. 1923, 166.
Berlin, Isaiah. *Fathers and Children.* Oxford, 1972.
Bialyi, G. A. "O psikhologicheskoi manere Turgeneva (Turgenev i Dostoevskii)," *Russkaia literatura,* No. 4, 1968, 34-50.
Bialyi, G. A. *Roman Turgeneva "Ottsy i deti."* M-L. l963. 2nd edition, 1968.
Bialyi, G. A. *Turgenev i russkii realizm.* M-L. 1962, 112-171.
Bialyi, G.A. "V. Arkhipov protiv Turgeneva," *Novyi mir,* No. 8, 1958, 255-259.
Blair, Joel. "The Architecture of Turgenev's *Fathers and Sons," Modern Fiction Studies,* Vol. XIX, No. 4, 1973-74, 555-563.
Bourget, Paul. "Ivan Tourguénev," *Essais de psychologie contemporaine.* Paris, 1920.
Boyd, Alexander F. "A Landscape with Figures: Ivan Turgenev and *Fathers and Sons," Aspects of the Russian Novel.* Totawa, New Jersey, 1972, 68-86.
Brazhe, T. G. *Tselostnoe izuchenie epicheskogo proizvedeniia.* M. 1964, 18-119.
Brodskii, N. L. "O romane *Ottsy i deti,"* in I. S. Turgenev, *Ottsy i deti.* M. 1967, 200-208.
Brodskii, N. L. "Obzor turgenevskoi iubileinoi literatury," *Nauchnye izvestiia, sbornik vtoroi.* M, 1922. 208-209.
Brodskii, N. L. *Zamysly I. S. Turgeneva.* M. 1917.
Brumfield, William C. "Bazarov and Rjazanov: The Romantic Archetype in Russian Nihilism," *Slavic and East European Journal,* XXI, 4 (1977), 499-505.
Budanova, N. F. "Problema 'ottsov' i 'detei' v romane *Besy," Dostoevskii: Materialy i issledovaniia,* ed. G. M. Fridlender. L. 1974, 164-188.
Burns, Virginia M. "The Structure of the Plot of *Ottsy i deti," Russian Literature,* No. 6, 1974, 33-53.
Chernov, N. M. "Ob odnom znakomstve I. S. Turgeneva," *Voprosy literatury,* No. 8, 1961, 188-193.
Chernyshev, K. *Lishnie liudi i zhenskie tipy v romanakh i povestiakh I. S. Turgeneva.* M-St.P. 1913.
Chukovskii, K. *Liudi i knigi shestidesiatykh godov.* L. 1934.
D'iakonov, V. I. "Sravneniia Turgeneva," *Turgenev i ego vremia,* ed. N. L.

Brodskii. M-Pg. 1923, 77-141.

Dolinin, A. S. "Turgenev v *Besakh,*" *F. M. Dostoevskii. Stat'i i materialy. Sbornik 2,* ed. A. S. Dolinin. M-L. 1924, 119-136.

Edgerton, W. B. "I. S. Turgenev i spornyi vopros o Iakushkinykh," *Russkaia literatura,* No. 1, 1967, 149-154.

Eliason, Lynn R. "A Nineteenth-Century Solution to the Problem of the Generations—Turgenev and Theodore Fontane," *Germano-Slavica,* No. 2, 1973, 29-34.

Evgen'ev-Maksimov, V. *N. A. Nekrasov i ego sovremenniki.* M. 1930, 99-176.

Fischler, Alexander. "The Garden Motif and the Structure of Turgenev's *Fathers and Sons,*" *Novel,* 9 (1976), 245-255.

Fridlender, G. M. "K sporam ob *Ottsakh i detiakh,*" *Russkaia literatura,* No. 2, 1959, 131-148.

Garnett, Edward. *Turgenev.* Port Washington, New York, 1924.

Gershenzon, M. *Mechta i mysl' I. S. Turgeneva.* M. 1919.

Gifford, Henry. *The Hero of His Time. A Theme in Russian Literature.* London, 1950.

Gifford, Henry. "Turgenev," in *Nineteenth-Century Russian Literature,* ed. John Fennell. Berkeley, 1973, 143-167.

Gippius, Vasilii. "O kompozitsii turgenevskikh romanov," in *Venok Turgenevu.* Odessa, 1919, 25-55.

Granjard, Henri. *Ivan Tourguénev et les courants politiques et sociaux de son temps.* Paris, 1953. 2nd edition, 1966.

Grazhis, P. I. *Turgenev i russkii romantizm.* Kazan, 1966.

Gruzinskii, A. E. *I. S. Turgenev.* M. 1918, 153-159.

Hart, Pierre. "Nature as the Norm in *Ottsy i Deti,*" *Russian Language Journal,* No. 110 (1977), 55-64.

Haumant, Emile. *Ivan Tourguénev: la vie et l'oeuvre.* Paris, 1905.

Hershkowitz, Harry. *Democratic Ideas in Turgenev's Works.* New York, 1932.

Herzen, A. I. "Eshche raz Bazarov," in A. I. Herzen, *Polnoe sobranie sochinenii i pisem,* Vol. XXI, ed. M. K. Lemke. M-Pg. 1923, 224-238.

Hindus, Milton. "The Duels in Mann and Turgenev," *Comparative Literature,* Vol. XI, 1959, 303-312.

Howe, Irving. "Turgenev: The Politics of Hesitation," *Politics and the Novel.* London, 1961, 114-138.

Ingham, Norman. "Turgenev in the Garden," in *Mnemozina,* ed. Joachim T. Baer and Norman W. Ingham. Munich. 1974, 224.

Jahn, Gary R. "Character and Theme in *Fathers and Sons.*" *College Literature,* 4 (1977), 80-91.

Justus, James H. "*Fathers and Sons:* The Novel as Idyll," *Western Humanities Review,* Vol. XV, 1961, 259-265.

Kagan-Kans, Eva. *Hamlet and Don Quixote: Turgenev's Ambivalent Vision.* The Hague, 1975.

Kin, V. P. "Gamletizm i nigilizm v tvorchestve Turgeneva," *Literatura i marksizm,* Book VI, 1929, 71-116.

Kleman, M. K. *Ivan Sergeevich Turgenev: ocherk zhizni i tvorchestva.* L. 1936.

Kleman, M. K. "I. S. Turgenev v rabote nad romanom," *Literaturnaia ucheba,* No. 5, 1933, 23-49.

Kleman, M. K. *Letopis' zhizni i tvorchestva I. S. Turgeneva.* M-L. 1934.

Klevenskii, M. M. "Obshchestvenno-politicheskie vzgliady I. S. Turgeneva," *Tvorchestvo Turgeneva,* eds. I. U. Rozanov and Iu. M. Sokolov. M. 1920, 168-193.

Kovalevskii, M. M. "Vospominaniia ob I. S. Turgeneve," *Minuvshie gody,* No. 8, 1908, 14.

Koz'min, B. P. "Dva slova o slove 'nigilizm'," *Izvestiia AN SSSR,* Otdelenie literatury i iazyka, Vol X, vyp. 4, 1951, 378-385.

Kurliandskaia, G. B. *Khudozhestvennyi metod Turgeneva-romanista.* Tula, 1972.

Loshchinin, P. N. "Roman *Ottsy i deti,*" *Tvorchestvo I. S. Turgeneva,* ed. S. M. Petrov. M. 1958, 298-343.

Lowe, David A. "Comedy and Tragedy in *Fathers and Sons*: A Structural Analysis," *Canadian-American Slavic Studies,* XIII, 3, 1979, 283-294.

Lowe, David A. *"Otcy i deti* and Turgenev's Correspondence: A Study in Reciprocity," *Russian Language Journal,* XXXIII, No. 114, 1979, 55-62.

Lunacharskii, A. V. "Literatura shestidesiatykh godov," *Russkaia literatura.* M. 1947, 83-99.

L'vov-Rogachevskii, V. L. "Bor'ba pokolenii (*Ottsy i deti* Turgeneva)," *Rabochii mir,* Nos. 12-13, 1918, 30-35.

Magarshack, David. *Turgenev: A Life.* London. 1954.

Mann, Iu. "Bazarov i drugie," *Novyi mir,* Vol. 44, No. 10, 1968, 236-255.

Matlaw, Ralph E. "Turgenev's Novels and *Fathers and Sons,*" in Ivan Turgenev, *Fathers and Sons: The Author on the Novel, Contemporary Reactions, Essays in Criticism,* ed. Ralph E. Matlaw. New York, 1966, 261-278.

Matlaw, Ralph E. "Turgenev's Novels: Civic Responsibility and Literary Predilection," *Harvard Slavic Studies,* Vol. IV, 1957, 249-262.

Mazon, A. *Manuscrits parisiens d'Ivan Tourguénev: notices et extraits.* Paris, 1930.

Mazon, A. *Parizhskie rukopisi I. S. Turgeneva.* M-L. 1931. (This is a translation of the work listed in the preceding citation.)

Mel'nik, V. I. "Istochnik odnoi repliki Bazarova," *Russkaia literatura,* XX, i, 1974, 173-175.

Mirsky, D. S. *A History of Russian Literature from Its Beginnings to 1900,* ed. Francis J. Whitfield. New York, 1958.

Moser, Charles A. *Antinihilism in the Russian Novel of the 1860s.* The Hague, 1964.

Moser, Charles A. *Ivan Turgenev.* New York, 1972.

Muchnic, Helen. *An Introduction to Russian Literature.* New York, 1947, 125-149.

Nierle, Michael. *Die Naturschilderung und ihre Funktionen in Versdichtung und Prosa von I. S. Turgenev.* Bad Homburg v. d. H., 1969, 246-250.

Nikol'skii, Iurii. *Turgenev i Dostoevskii: istoriia odnoi vrazhdy.* Sofia, 1921.

Ostrovskaia, N. A. "Vospominaniia N. A. Ostrovskoi," *I. S. Turgenev v vospominaniiakh sovremennikov i ego pis'makh.* Vol I. M. 1924, 67-68.

Ovsianiko-Kulikovskii, D. N. *Stat'i o Bazarove i o ego vremeni.* M. 1924.

Panaeva, A. Ia. *Vospominaniia.* M. 1972, 125.

Peterson, Dale. *The Clement Vision: Poetic Realism in Turgenev and James.* Port Washington, New York, 1975.

Petrov, S. *Turgenev: zhizn' i tvorchetsvo.* M. 1968.

Petrovskii, M. A. "Tainstvennoe u Turgeneva," *Tvorchestvo Turgeneva,* eds. I. U. Rozanov and Iu. M. Sokolov. M. 1920, 70-89.

Piksanov, N. K. "Velikoe nasledie Turgeneva," *I. S. Turgenev: materialy i issledovaniia,* ed. N. L. Brodskii. Orel, 1940, 74.

Pisarev, D. I. "Bazarov," *Bazarov; Realisty.* M. 1974, 5-72.

Pisarev, D. I. "Realisty," *Bazarov; Realisty.* M. 1974, 75-282.

Polovtsev, A. I. "Vospominaniia," *Russkie pisateli o literaturnom trude.* Vol. II. M. 1955, 753.

Pritchett, V. S. *The Gentle Barbarian: The Life and Work of Turgenev.* New York, 1977.

Pustovoit, P. G. *Ivan Sergeevich Turgenev.* M. 1957.

Pustovoit, P. G. *Roman I. S. Turgeneva "Ottsy i deti" i ideinaia bor'ba 60-kh godov XIX veka.* M. 1960.

Pustovoit, P. G. *Roman I. S. Turgeneva "Ottsy i deti." Literaturnye kommentarii.* M. 1964.

Reeve, F. D. "Fathers and Children," *The Russian Novel.* New York, 1966, 119-158.

Sabliovskii, P. V. "Iazyk Bazarova," *Rodnoi iazyk v shkole,* No 9, 1926, 51.

Schapiro, Leonard. *Turgenev: His Life and Times.* New York. 1978, 176-190.

Seeley, Frank F. "Theme and Structure in *Fathers and Sons,*" *Annali,* Sezione Slava, XII (Naples, 1970), 83-104.

Shklovskii, V. *Zametki o proze russkikh klassikov.* M. 1955, 200-222.

Sokolov, B. M. "Muzhiki v izobrazhenii Turgeneva," *Tvorchestvo Turgeneva,* eds. I. U. Rozanov and Iu. M. Sokolov. M. 1920, 194-233.

Strakhov, N. N. *"Ottsy i deti,"* *Vremia,* No. 4, 1862.

Terras, Victor. "Turgenev's Aesthetic and Western Realism," *Comparative Literature,* No. 22, 1970, 19-35.

Tiun'kin, K. I. "Bazarov glazami Dostoevskogo," *Dostoevskii i ego vremia.* L. 1971, 108-119.

Trautman, Reinhold. *Turgenjew Novelist.* Leipzig. 1948.

Veksler, I. *Turgenev i politicheskaia bor'ba 60-kh godov.* M-L. 1935.
Vinnikova, Galina. *Turgenev i Rossiia.* M. 1971.
Vinogradov, I. A. *Bor'ba za stil': sbornik statei.* L. 1937, 192-199.
Vodovozova, E. N. *Na zare zhizni.* Spb. 1911, 459, 521.
Wellek, Rene. "Fathers and Sons," in *World Masterpieces,* ed. Maynard Mack. Vol. II. New York, 1965, 658-662.
Wilson, Edmund. "Turgenev and the Life-Giving Drop," *A Window on Russia.* New York, 1972, 68-147.
Yarmolinsky, Avrahm. *Turgenev: The Man, His Art and His Age.* New York, 1961.
Zacharkin, Adrzej. "Prolematyka szczęścia i obowiązku w twórczosći Iwana Turgieniewa," *Slavia Orientalis,* No. 18, 1969, 243-252.

OTHER WORKS CITED IN THE MONOGRAPH:

Bakhtin, M. *Problemy poetiki Dostoevskogo.* 3rd edition. M. 1972.
Billington, James H. *The Icon and the Axe: An Interpretive History of Russian Culture.* New York, 1970.
Byron, George Lord. *Works of Lord Byron.* New York, 1970.
Chernyshevskii, N. G. *Polnoe sobranie sochinenii v 15- tomakh.* M. 1950.
Dobroliubov, N. A. *Sobranie sochinenii v 9-i tomakh.* M-L. 1962.
Dostoevskii, F. M. *Polnoe sobranie sochinenii.* L. 1972.
Dostoevskii, F. M. *Pis'ma,* ed. by A. S. Dolinin. M. 1930.
Ehre, Milton. *Oblomov and His Creator: The Life and Art of Ivan Goncharov.* Princeton, 1973.
Eikhenbaum, B. M. *Lev Tolstoi.* L. 1928/31.
Eizenshtein, Sergei. *Izbrannye proizvedeniia v 6-i tomakh.* M. 1964.
Fet, A. *Moi vospominaniia.* M. 1890.
Frye, Northrop. *Anatomy of Criticism.* Princeton, 1957.
Herzen, A. I. *Sobranie sochinenii v 30-i tomakh.* M. 1963.
Lampert, E. *Sons Against Fathers.* Oxford, 1965.
Ledkovsky, Marina. *The Other Turgenev: From Romanticism to Symbolism.* Wurzburg, 1973.
Malia, Martin. "What Is the Intelligentsia?", *The Russian Intelligentsia,* ed. Richard Pipes. New York, 1961.
Pisarev, D. I. *Sochineniia v 4-kh tomakh.* M. 1955.
Praz, Mario. *The Romantic Agony,* trans. Angus Davidson. New York, 1951.
Steiner, George. *Tolstoy or Dostoevsky: An Essay in the Old Criticism.* New York, 1959.
Van Schooneveld, C. H. "Gogol' and the Romantics," in *Essays in Honor of Kiril Taranovsky,* eds. Roman Jakobson, C. H. van Schooneveld, Dean S. Worth. The Hague, 1973, 481-484.
Walicki, A. "Turgenev and Schopenhauer," *Oxford Slavonic Papers,* X, 1962.